HINDUISM
Sacred Texts
Vedas, Upanishads, Āgamas, Purānas,...

HINDUISM
Sacred Texts
Vedas, Upanishads, Āgamas, Purānas,...

By
Sadhu Vivekjivandas

Editorial Consultant
Dr Janakbhai Dave

Swaminarayan Aksharpith
Ahmedabad

HINDUISM
Sacred Texts

Inspirer: HDH Pramukh Swami Maharaj

1st Edition: April 2013

Copies: 7,000

Price: ₹ 55/-

ISBN: 978-81-7526-361-1

Published & Printed by
Swaminarayan Aksharpith
Shahibaug Road, Ahmedabad-4
Gujarat, India.

Websites: www.baps.org

CONTENTS

$1.50

PREFACE

The sacred texts of Sanātana Dharma or Hinduism are known as 'shastras'. The word 'shastra' means a treatise that commands and protects the person who abides by it. In addition, the shastras deal with the life and teachings of Paramātmā (God) and his avatars (incarnations).

Hinduism has a rich legacy of spiritual wisdom and history in the form of its sacred texts: Vedas, Upanishads, Dharma Shastras, Āgamas, Purānas, Rāmāyana, Mahābhārata, etc. The Vedas hold the pride of place among all Hindu shastras, besides being the oldest. They were revealed by Paramātmā to enlightened rishis. They are called the Shruti shastras. 'Shruti' means that which was 'heard' or revealed. The Shruti shastras are the primary sacred texts of Hinduism, which were not man-made (*apaurusheya*). They contain prayers to devas or personified forces of nature and the Ultimate Reality. They also comprise of *yajna* rituals, spiritual interpretation of rituals, and philosophical discourses on the nature of Paramātmā, the soul and the world.

The chronological and philosophical culminations of

the Vedas are called the Upanishads. The Upanishads are mainly philosophical and theological dialogues that encompass the nature and functions of Parabrahman, Brahman, *jiva* (soul), *jagat* (world), *mukti* (liberation), etc.

The secondary sacred texts in Hinduism are known as Smruti shastras. 'Smruti' means that which was 'remembered'. They are a repository of Hindu knowledge and history. They were written by great seers, based on the teachings they remembered from their spiritual masters. This branch includes the Dharma Shastras (social and moral codes of conduct such as Manu Smruti, etc.), the Itihāsa or epics (Rāmāyana and Mahābhārata), and the Purānas (ancient religious and historical literature).

In addition, the Vedic literature and sciences consist of Vedāngas (limbs of Vedas) and Upavedas (subsidiary Vedas), the Āgamas and the Sutra literature. These are an important part of the corpus of Hindu shastras. The Vedāngas assist in studying, reciting, understanding and practising the teachings of the Vedas. The Upavedas deal with secular arts and sciences like music, dance, warfare, architecture and medicine. The Āgamas concern themselves with philosophy, yogic practices, mandir architecture, consecration of *murti,* rituals and codes of conduct. The Sutra literature consists of brief statements or aphorisms. They can be called the shorthand of the Hindu shastras.

The principal aims of all the Hindu shastras are to inspire faith, character and peace, attain happiness in this world and achieve the final goal of life – *moksha*. They therefore teach and prescribe social, moral and spiritual principles.

Daily reading and study of the sacred texts encourage sound moral behaviour, spiritual knowledge and enlightenment in one's life.

Hinduism, Sacred Texts is mainly sourced from *Hinduism, An Introduction, Part 1,* published by Swaminarayan Aksharpith. This publication briefly informs the reader about the Vedas, Upanishads, Dharma Shastras, Āgamas, Purānas, Itihāsa, Vedic Literature and Sciences. The three additional chapters in this book are on the Vachanāmrut (spiritual teachings of Bhagwan Swaminarayan), FAQs and the reflections of scholars on the Hindu sacred texts.

I am deeply thankful to H.H. Pramukh Swami Maharaj for his blessings and inspiration which enabled me to write this book. And my appreciations to Pujya Ishwarcharan Swami for his motivation and guidance, Dr Janakbhai

Dave for resolving textual errors and doubts, and Pujya Amrutvijay Swami and Shri Varanasi Rama Murthy for reviewing the language and content of the text.

Every Hindu and spiritual seeker interested in Hindu Dharma may profitably read this book to understand the profound spiritual wisdom and glory of the ancient Sanātana Dharma.

- **Author**

From top: Sacred manuscripts of Rig, Yajur, Sāma and Atharva Vedas

1. VEDAS AND UPANISHADS

INTRODUCTION

The sacred texts or scriptures that contain the tenets of Hindu Dharma are called shastras. The word 'shastra' literally means a treatise that commands and protects the person who obeys it. Furthermore, shastra also includes works on the life stories and teachings of the avatars of Paramātmā or God.

Hinduism has a rich collection of shastras, namely, the Vedas or Shruti shastras, Smruti shastras, Agamas and Tantras, Vedāngas, Upavedas and Sutra literature. For many Hindus the holiest and the most ancient of shastras are the Vedas or Shrutis. Shruti means "that which is heard" or revealed. They were revealed by Paramātmā or God to the ancient rishis in their deep meditation. Then the Vedas or the revealed knowledge was handed down by an oral tradition. In the broader sense the Vedas include the four Samhitās, Brāhmana texts, the Āranyaka texts and the Upanishads. The latter three have their roots and sources in the four Samhitās. The four Samhitās are the Rig, Yajur, Sāma and

Atharva Samhitās. The Samhitās primarily comprise of prayers to personified natural forces or devas like fire, rain, water, thunder, etc., and the Ultimate Reality. They deal with prayers for prosperity, progeny, matrimony, domestic rites and more. The Brāhmana texts provide explanation of and guidance for *yajna* rituals and other things, and the Āranyakas include spiritual contemplation and meditation. The Upanishads contain philosophical and theological discourses on Brahman (Ultimate Reality) and its relation to souls and the material world. Traditional schools of Hinduism consider the Vedas to be the most authoritative sacred texts.

In addition to the Shruti shastras, there are texts known as Smruti. Although they are secondary in authority to the Vedas, the Smruti shastras also play a very important role in Hinduism. 'Smruti' means "that which is remembered". Smruti shastras are the written accounts of rishis who remembered what they had heard from their great spiritual masters. As opposed to Shruti shastras, Smruti shastras were composed through human agency. They deal with moral and social laws, rites and rituals and history. They include the body of texts known as Dharma Shastras such as Manu Smruti, Yājnavalkya Smruti, etc., Itihāsa or epics, namely, the Rāmāyana and Mahābhārata (with the Bhagavad Gitā as its core), and the 18 Mahā-Purānas, 18 Upa-Purānas and other literature.

Both the *shrutis* and *smrutis* deal with the ritual, philosophical, spiritual, moral and social aspects of Hinduism. They answer questions like who is God; where does he reside; what does he look like; how are we related to him; and how should we strive to realize him? They prescribe various means of realizing God, overcoming obstacles and the dos and don'ts of social and spiritual life.

The Āgamas or sectarian literature are exclusive to some *sampradāyas*. Their followers consider them to be divinely revealed *(shruti)* and equal in authority to the Vedas. The three Hindu traditions of Vaishnavism, Shaivism and Shāktism have their own Āgamas or Tantras (literature primarily devoted to Shakti or the Divine Mother). Even Buddhists and Jains have their own Āgamas or Tantras. The Vaishnava texts are called Vaishnava Āgamas, Shaivite texts are called Shaiva Āgamas and the Shākta texts are called Shākta Āgamas. The Āgamas deal mainly with the concept of God and the means to attain him through bhakti, rituals, ceremonies, construction of mandir, installation of sacred images, yoga and philosophy.

The Vedic sciences include the Vedāngas (limbs of the Vedas) and the Upavedas (subsidiary Vedas).

The Sutra literature is also a part of the ancient Sanskrit literature that contains concise statements of wisdom called *sutras* or aphorisms. It includes the Kalpasutras, Gruhyasutras and Brahmasutras.

According to the Purva Mimānsā (a school of philosophy which deals with the dos and don'ts, Vedic rites, rituals and sacrifices) and Uttara Mimānsā (or Vedānta, which deals with the topics of *ātmā,* Paramātmā, *jnāna* and *moksha)* a shastra should have four basic factors, viz:

1. *Vishaya* or a designated subject to discuss and inform.
2. *Prayojana* or purpose or goal to be gained by its study and practice.
3. *Sambandha* or connection with other related subjects.
4. *Adhikāri* means a competent student or person. So, a shastra is meant for one who is spiritually competent. The incompetent may misunderstand and misinterpret the shastra.

We shall now deal briefly with the Shruti texts – the Vedas, Brāhmanas, Āranyakas and the Upanishads. The other texts mentioned above will be dealt with in the subsequent chapters.

1. THE VEDAS (SHRUTI SHASTRAS)

The foundational shastra for all *āstika* Hindus are the

A Hindu believes in the authority and sanctity of the four Vedas and other sacred literature

Vedas. A practising Hindu is generally defined to be one who believes in the authority and sanctity of the Vedas.

The name Veda comes from the Sanskrit root word 'vid', which means 'to know'. Thus, the Vedas mean knowledge. They contain both spiritual and worldly knowledge. The Vedas are considered by Hindus to be the oldest sacred texts in the world which continue to be recited and studied to this day. Hindus consider the Vedas to be *apaurusheya*, i.e., not man-made, and revealed by God. It is difficult to assign a time frame for the Vedas. The dates given by different scholars range from 25000 BCE to 1000 BCE. Hindus regard the Vedas to be eternal.

Traditionally, the single large Veda was later classified

by Veda Vyāsa into four texts, namely, the Rig Veda, Yajur Veda (Krishna Yajur Veda and Shukla Yajur Veda), Sāma Veda and Atharva Veda. He taught one of them to each of his four disciples – Rig Veda to Paila, the Yajur Veda to Vaishampāyana, the Sāma Veda to Jaimini and the Atharva Veda to Sumantu.[1]

For millennia, the Vedas have been handed down to posterity by word of mouth. The Shruti texts or the Vedas, as traditionally defined, include the Samhitās, Brāhmanas, Āranyakas and Upanishads. Conventionally, it is the Samhitā (collection of mantras or hymns) that is indicated by the word Veda. There are four Samhitās, namely, Rik Samhitā or Rig Veda, Sāman Samhitā or Sāma Veda, Yajus Samhitā or Yajur Veda and Atharvan Samhitā or Atharva Veda. The Brāhmanas, the Āranyakas and the Upanishads of each of the four Vedic Samhitās have different names.

Each Samhitā has its own associated texts in prose called the Brāhmanas (which are ceremonial handbooks describing rules for rituals and explanations about its meaning), Āranyakas (deal with profound interpretations of rituals) and Upanishads (give metaphysical explanations). The Brāhmanas deal mainly with rules and regulations laid down for the performance of rites

---

1. Mahābhārata, Ādi Parva, 60.5 and Shrimad Bhāgavata, 12.6.50.

Veda Mandir, Ahmedabad

Murti of Veda Bhagwan worshipped
at Veda Mandir, Ahmedabad

and rituals of various *yajnas* (fire rituals, also known as sacrifices) as well as application of hymns in them. It also has interesting dialogues, myths and stories, but very little philosophy. The Samhitā and Brāhmana texts form the karma or ritual part (*karma-kānda*) of Vedic literature.

The Brāhmanas were followed by the Āranyaka texts, which were the result of contemplations of yogis and rishis in the forest. They mark the transition from ritualism to spiritualism, i.e., they discuss the spiritual significance of Vedic *yajnas* and devas. Finally, the Upanishads contain the very core of Indian philosophy (*jnāna-kānda*) and focus on the nature and relation between *jagat* (world), atman, Brahman (God) and *mukti* (liberation). They are the creative part of Indian Philosophy. They are also known as Vedānta because chronologically they form the "end" or "concluding" part of the Vedas, and philosophically they teach the highest spiritual knowledge. As their authority is unquestioned the Upanishads form the first of the three basic treatises of Vedānta called Prasthāntraya. Since the Upanishads are part of the Vedas they are also called Shrutiprasthāna. The Āranyaka and the Upanishad texts together form the *jnāna-kānda* or the knowledge section of the Vedas.

THE FOUR VEDAS OR VEDIC SAMHITĀS
I. RIG VEDA

The Rig Veda or Rig Veda Samhitā is the oldest and the most important of the four Vedas. It consists of ten *mandalas* (books), which have 1,028 *suktas* or *ruchās* (hymns) comprising of 10,552 mantras known as *ruks* (verses) that were revealed to various rishis at different periods of time. The mantras are prayers mainly to the nature gods to grant riches, progeny, long life, peace, and eternal happiness; and some mantras refer to victories of princes and kings in wars, subjects like marriage, generosity and other mundane things. The main devas or gods of the Rig Veda were Agni (fire-god), Indra (rain-god), Varuna (ocean-god), Mitra (sun-god),

A manuscript of the Rig Veda. It contains rituals for yajnas, prayers, philosophy, cosmology, process of creation,...

Vāyu (wind-god), Prajāpati (creator) and the Ashwins (divine physicians). The Rig Veda also has mantras like the *Nāsadiyasukta* and *Purushasukta* that are concerned with cosmology and creation. The Rig Veda contains philosophical ideas that form the basis of later philosophies derived and developed by the rishis. Bhakti or devotion also has its origin in the Rig Veda Samhitā. It teaches monotheism or belief in one Supreme Reality who is called by different names. The worship of the Supreme Reality having a form and qualities *(saguna upāsanā)* is also referred to in the Rig Veda. The Aitareya and Kaushitaki Āranyakas and Upanishads were developments from the Rig Veda.

The Vedic rishis were both male and female. Some of

Students reciting Vedic mantras in a gurukula,
Ved Vignan Maha Vidya Peeth, Bangalore

the prominent male rishis included Angiras, Agastya, Vasishtha, Vishwāmitra, Grutsamada. The main female rishis were Ghoshā, Godhā, Apālā, Kuhu, Sarama and others.

The special priest of the Rig Veda is called a *hotā*. He is an expert who recites the mantras of the Rig Veda to invoke the devas for receiving the oblations.

The mantras of the Rig Veda are in Vedic Sanskrit. For thousands of years these mantras have been meticulously transmitted orally, and finally when they came to be first written in the last few millennia, they were inscribed on dried palm leaves. Consequently, for thousands of years up to the present, there has been almost no change or corruption in the chanting and meaning of the Vedic mantras. There are, however, very minor variations in the written versions and even in oral versions owing to regional differences, transcription

A Yajur Veda manuscript. It deals mainly with rituals of worship

mistakes, and what might fall into the category of "human error".

II. YAJUR VEDA

The Yajur Veda mantras deal with the rituals of worship or the ceremonial aspect of Hinduism. There are about 1,975 mantras known as *yajus* that explain the significance of the performance of sacrificial rites. Many of the Yajur Veda mantras are found in the Rig Veda. The two branches of Yajur Veda are Krishna Yajur Veda and Shukla Yajur Veda. The former has both prose and poetry while the latter has only poetry. The language of the Yajur Veda and its descriptions of devas and society are very similar to that of the Rig Veda. There are a large number of mantras connected with *yajnas* like Ashvamedha, Vājapeya and Rājsuya. There are also mantras related to devotion in the Yajur Veda.

A part of *Sāma Veda* manuscript.
It is the Veda of music

The special priest of the Yajur Veda is known as *adhvaryu*. He is an expert in reciting mantras for specific rituals in *yajnas*.

The Taittiriya and Shatapatha Brāhmanas and Brihadāranyaka and Ishāvāsya Upanishads were a development from the Yajur Veda.

III. SĀMA VEDA

'Sāman' means 'tune', and in this case it refers to the tunes in which the Vedic hymns are chanted. The *sāmans* are essentially Rig Vedic mantras set to music. The Sāma Veda is also known as the Veda of music because all the mantras are set to the seven basic notes of Indian music known as the *sapta svara* system. The Sāma Veda is the smallest of the Vedas, but it is most appealing because of its sweet music, poetic expression and touching sentiments of devotion. It is believed that the birth of Indian classical music can be traced to the Sāma Veda.

The Sāma Veda has 1,875 mantras, the majority of which are from the Rig Veda. The Panchavimsha, and Shadvimsha Brāhmanas, the Tāndya, Chāndogya and Kena Upanishads were a development from the Sāma Veda.

The Sāma Veda gained importance and prominence because Bhagwan Krishna said in the Bhagavad Gitā (10.22), "I am Sāma Veda among the Vedas."

The special priest of Sāma Veda is known as an *udgātā*. He is an expert singer who invites the devas by singing the mantras to entertain and please them.

A part of Atharva Veda manuscript. It deals with health, victory, friendship, charms, and chants used in warfare

IV. ATHARVA VEDA

The Atharva Veda was not included as the Fourth Veda up to the time of the Bhagavad Gitā[2], because its mantras had little to do with the main *yajna* rituals as in the other three Vedas. It has information on aspects that are not found in the other three Vedas. The Atharva Veda contains 736 hymns or *suktas* with a total of 6,077 mantras. They deal with health, medicine, victory, friendship, progeny, black magic, and charms and chants used for offensive and defensive purposes.

2. The Bhagavad Gitā mentions the three Vedas as *traividya* or *trayi* (B.G. 9. 20-21).

The Atharva Veda also contains mantras that deal with building construction, trade and commerce, statecraft, penances, long life, harmony in life and mantras to ward off evil spirits. This Veda also refers to *swarga* (heaven) and *naraka* (hell), virtue and sin, and qualities like *satya* (truth) and *tapas* (austerity), and ceremony like *dikshā* (initiation) that help a person attain perfection.

The Atharva Veda is also called Brahmā Veda because the priests who specialise in its recitation are called the Brahmā priests. Furthermore it is also called Bhaishajya Veda (the Veda of medicines and treatment of diseases) and Kshattra Veda (the Veda of the warrior class). So, unlike the other Vedas, the Atharva Veda touches a wider scope of worldly subjects.

The Gopatha Brāhmana and three important Upanishads, Prashna, Mundaka and Māndukya, developed from it.

2. CONTENT OF VEDAS

The Vedas predominantly deal with prayers to the nature gods and the Ultimate Reality, the means to attain desirable objects and avoid undesirable ones. They generally elaborate upon devas (gods), and sometimes upon devis (goddesses), man, morality, rituals to propitiate devas, unity of all beings and *moksha*. They also deal with matrimony, friendship, prayers, progeny, longevity, prosperity and medicines.

The Rig Veda is revered and recited by Hindus

Chanting of mantras as prayers by individuals was the first stage in the Vedic period (Samhitā period). During this time an individual himself chanted prayers for his spiritual and secular progress. He himself was both the host and the priest for all his rituals, prayers and worship. The *yajna* rituals represented the second stage (Brāhmana period) wherein a householder performed different and elaborate *yajna* rituals under the guidance and instruction of specialist priests. The third stage (Āranyaka period) emphasized meditation and contemplation on the concept of *yajna* rituals. In this there was almost no actual performance of the rituals. This stage was a link between the ritualism of the Brāhmana period and the philosophy of the Upanishadic period. And, the final and fourth stage was the Upanishadic period wherein the guru taught his disciples the esoteric doctrine of Paramātmā, *ātmā*, creation of world, *moksha* and other metaphysical subjects. This constituted the *jnā-*

Ruta is the principle of cosmic order

na-mārga or path of knowledge for *moksha*.

The gradual shift in focus from ritualism to spiritualism through the Vedic periods thus sought to satisfy all the needs and wants of man, whether mundane or transcendental. Some very important principles and rituals are given in the Vedas, including *ruta* (cosmic order), *satya* (here: moral order), *runa* (obligation), hymns of creation *(Nāsadiyasukta)* and the Ultimate Reality *(Purushasukta)*. They are briefly discussed below.

1. RUTA (COSMIC ORDER)

Ruta is the universal principle of cosmic order or laws of nature that prevail over or govern all the universes. *Ruta* is mentioned in the Rig Veda and Krishna Yajur Veda, and it is one of the important concepts of Sanātana Dharma. *Ruta* pervades all of creation, and must be observed by all the devas and humans. The whole universe is founded on *ruta* and moves in it. Prof. Gavin Flood writes, "This integration of society and cosmos, of body and society, is sacred order or law *(ruta)* of the universe, which is eternal and unchanging, brought to life in vedic ritual, expressed in the songs of the vedic seers, and elucidated in the Brāhmanas [texts]."[3] Varuna deva is both the custodian of *ruta* and *satya*.

Prayers being offered to the sun-god

II. SATYA (MORAL ORDER)

Satya or truth is the universal moral order that applies to all human beings. It is the essential characteristic of Paramātmā and therefore *satya* stands for God. *Satya* is unchanging and unaffected by time and place; it is eternal. Abiding by *satya* one always triumphs and attains spiritual elevation. *Satya* helps a person progress towards God. The Mundaka Upanishad states, *"Satyam eva jayate na anrutam"* – "Only truth triumphs not untruth."[4] The first half, *"Satyam eva jayate,"* is the motto of the Government of India.

III. RUNA (OBLIGATION)

Another important concept is that of *runa*, which

3. Flood, Gavin. *An Introduction to Hinduism.* New Delhi: Cambridge University Press, Foundation Books, First South Asian Edition, 2004, p. 49.
4. Mundaka 3.1.6.

means indebtedness or obligation. Sanātana Dharma believes that man is indebted to the devas (gods), rishis, *pitrus* (forefathers), people and animals in many ways. *Runa* is hinted at in the Rig Veda (8. 32.16 and 6. 61.1), and stated clearly in the Taittiriya Samhitā (6. 3.10.5) of the Krishna Yajur Veda and the Shatapatha Brāhmana text of Shukla Yajur Veda (1. 7.2.11). The concept is first described as *runa-traya* (three-fold debts or obligations), namely, *deva-runa* (debt to gods), *rishi-runa* (debt to sages) and *pitru runa* (debt to ancestors). Later two more obligations were added to form the five *runas*, i.e., *nru-runa* (debt to human beings) and *bhuta-runa* (debt to all living beings including birds, animals, etc.).[5] It is to be noted that the five *runas* or obligations are fulfilled through the practice of *panchamahāyajnas*, namely, *deva-yajna, rishi-yajna, pitru-yajna, nru-yajna* and *bhuta-yajna*. The word *yajna*, with the exception of *deva-yajna,* does not refer to performance of fire sacrifices, but alludes to selfless religious and charitable services performed to repay one's debts. Hence, the Hindu shastras prescribe the performances of *panchamahāyajnas* by all householders. Let us consider each of the *runas* briefly.

1. **Deva-runa** means indebtedness to the devas (gods). The devas give us many things in the form of nature, like

---

5. Hiriyanna. M. *Outlines of Indian Philosophy.* London: George Allen & Unwin Ltd, 1951, p.45.

Deva-runa: Offering oblations to the devas in a yajna kunda

Rishi-runa: Studying and teaching the sacred texts

light, water, fire, air and wind. By offering oblations in a *yajna kunda* (fire altar) an aspirant expresses his appreciation to the devas and seeks their blessings for happiness, prosperity and protection. This is called *deva-yajna*. When the devas are pleased by the offerings, they make the natural forces helpful to the worshippers and also fulfil their worldly desires.

Thus *deva-runa* is repaid by properly performing Vedic sacrifices or *deva-yajnas*.

2. **Rishi-runa** means indebtedness to the rishis or sages, who gave us the legacy of spirituality, culture and education. This debt can be repaid by studying the sacred texts, teaching them to the next generation,

Pitru-runa: Offering rites to propitiate one's ancestors

Nru-runa: Charity and service to humanity

practising them and performing the samskaras and austerities prescribed by sages. This is called *rishi-yajna* or *brahma-yajna*.

3. ***Pitru-runa*** means obligation to one's forefathers. This is fulfilled by getting married, i.e., becoming a householder. One appeases one's ancestors by offering rice balls *(pindas)* and water *(arghya)* daily. Furthermore, it also includes performance of funeral rites and subsequently the annual *shrāddha* or rite to propitiate one's ancestors. The practice of these rites and rituals is known as *pitru-yajna*.

4. ***Nru-runa*** is the fourth obligation. It refers to charity to mankind and serving human beings who are ailing,

needy, in difficulty and in pain. Serving society in times of calamity and need is the fulfilment of *nru-runa*. It also includes the preservation of social, cultural and moral values by practising truth, kindness to fellow humans, and love for neighbours and friends.

Bhuta-runa: Offering food and service to and service to animals

God blesses those who fulfil *nru-runa* with peace, happiness and progress. The practice of these rituals is called *nru-yajna*.

5. **Bhuta-runa** is the last of the five human debts. In this, people are expected to repay it daily by setting apart a portion of their meals for the birds and animals. This ritual practice is called *bhuta-yajna*. Furthermore, the Mahābhārata mentions an important aspect of *bhuta-runa*: not to be cruel but to be kind to all living beings.[6]

The first and third (*deva-runa* and *pitru-runa*) deal mainly with sacrificial rites (*yajnas*), and the last two (*nru-runa* and *bhuta-runa*) deal mainly with acts of charity, sympathy and

---

6. Ādi Parva, 120. 17-20.

nonviolence. The *rishi-runa* deals with self-study, practising austerity and transmission of sacred texts to the next generation. Collectively these *runas* are known as *ishtāpurta,* which means the cumulative result of performance of sacrificial rites and good works for others.[7]

Through the principle of *runa* and the ritual of repaying debts, people learn to rise above self-centredness and to be grateful to all those from whom they obtain and inherit many things.

IV. HYMNS OF CREATION AND THE ULTIMATE REALITY

The Rig Veda has some of the best mystical poetic hymns, like the *Nāsadiyasukta* (hymn of creation: 10.129.1-7), and the *Purushasukta* (hymn of the Ultimate Reality: 10.90. 1-16). The *Nāsadiyasukta* deals with the difficult topic of creation. It describes what existed before creation and how creation came about through the Ultimate Reality. Briefly, the hymn says that the Ultimate Reality willed the creation of this world and the living and non-living forms got manifested. The whole secret of creation is known perhaps only to Him. The hymn states, "It is Positive Being from whom the whole existence arrives. The Absolute Reality is at the

---

7. Monier-Williams, Monier. *A Sanskrit-English Dictionary.* Clarendon, UK: OUP, 1988, p.169.

back of the whole world."[8] With regards to the origin of the universes the *Nāsadiyasukta* describes creation to have been willed by an external agency, i.e., the Ultimate Reality.

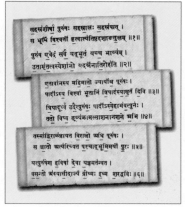

Purushasukta hymn, in praise of the Supreme Person, in the Rig Veda

The *Purushasukta* in the Rig Veda shows the organic and social unity of the universes. In this hymn, all existence – earth, heavens, devas, planets, living and non-living objects, four varnas, time and other aspects of society – originated from the Ultimate Reality (Purusha), who pervades the world and yet remains beyond it. So the Ultimate Reality is shown to be immanent and transcendent.

The belief in the one Ultimate Reality is the principle of these two hymns.

3. THE UPANISHADS

The Upanishads, also known as Vedānta, are the culmination of the Vedas, both philosophically and chronologically. The Upanishads form a part of the Shruti shastras. They

---

8. Radhakrishnan, S. *History of Indian Philosophy, Vol.1.* London: Allen & Unwin, 1948, p.101.

The Upanishads explain spiritual truths through dialogues, anecdotes, allegories and stories

have inspired and sustained the faith of the Hindus over the millennia. Swami Harshananda, a senior sanyasi and scholar of the Ramakrishna Order, writes, "By advocating the ultimate triumph of the spirit over matter, of man over nature, the Upanishads have created, strengthened and preserved a great tradition of spirituality.... No school of thought, no religious movement, of the subsequent periods in the history of India has remained untouched by their influence, if not pervaded by them."[9] The Upanishads are philosophical dialogues that contain the core of Vedic philosophy and thus form the fundamental *jnāna-kānda* of Hindu philosophy. They are independent and unique works by themselves

9. Swami Harshananda. *A Concise Encyclopaedia of Hinduism, Vol.3.* Bangalore: Ramakrishna Math, 2008, pp. 439-440.

Sacred manuscripts traditionally wrapped in cloth

Manuscript of Ishāvāsya Upanishad

in thought and sentiment despite their being the end-part of the Vedas. The emphasis from rituals and ceremonies prominent in the Brāhmanic period shifted to philosophy and spiritual wisdom from the Upanishadic period. Tradition asserts that there are more than 200 Upanishads. Among them ten are the oldest and prominent, on which Ādi Shankarachārya had written his commentaries. They are Isha, Kena, Katha, Prashna, Mundaka, Māndukya, Taittiriya, Aitareya, Chāndogya and Brihadāranyaka. Some also add three other ancient Upanishads, the Shvetāshvatara, Kaushitaki and Maitri, to this list of principal Upanishads.[10] The Upanishads explain the spiritual truths through dia-

10. Hume, Robert Ernest. *The Thirteen Principal Upanishads.* New York: OUP, 1975.

logues, anecdotes, allegories and stories.

The word Upanishad is derived from the root 'sad' which means 'to sit', with the prefixes 'upa' and 'ni' meaning 'very near'. Upanishad thus means 'to sit devotedly very near the guru' to listen to the sublime spiritual truths. The guru, through verbal instructions or mere presence, dissolves the doubts and ignorance of his disciples.

Four brief statements, considered by some Vedāntins to be the gist of the Upanishads, are known as the *mahāvākyas*. They are:

1. *"Prajnānam Brahma"* – "Divine Consciousness is the Supreme Reality" (Aitareya: 5.3).

2. *"Aham Brahmāsmi"* – "I am Brahman" (Brihadāranyaka: 1.4.10).

3. *"Tat tvam asi"* – "You are That (Brahman)" (Chāndogya: 6.8.7).

4. *"Ayam ātmā Brahma"* – "This indwelling self is Brahman" (Māndukya:2).

These four statements contain, in a nutshell, very important elements of Upanishadic philosophy. Then, through discussions, these philosophical statements later developed into many works of Vedānta, like the Mahāvākya Upanishad.

The Upanishadic knowledge of Brahman and Parabrahman, *jiva*, *jagat* and *mukti* was transmitted from generation to generation, in which each disciple after graduating was bound by duty to disseminate it to his sons or disciples.

In the long tradition of Vedic literature, the Upanishads represent the most earnest and sincere

Satyakāma Jābāla gains brahmavidyā through obedience to guru

efforts of the profound thinkers (sages and seers) to solve the problems of the origin, nature and destiny of man and the universe, and the meaning and value of 'knowing' and 'being'.

TEACHINGS

The Upanishads describe that our world (samsara) is ever changing and perishable. However, the Supreme Reality or Parabrahman, that pervades the world, is eternal and unchanging. He is the bedrock and essence of all things. The Mundaka Upanishad describes the pervasive nature of Parabrahman. The Upanishads confirm that though sages worshipped many manifestations of the Divine, there is only one underlying Parabrahman described variously by wise men as mentioned in the Rig Veda 1.164.45: *"Ekam sat viprāhā bahuddhā vadanti."* Everything comes from that Supreme Reality or through his will.

The Katha Upanishad states that the body is destroyed but not the *ātmā* and Paramātmā (God) that reside within it. The Chāndogya Upanishad says *"Tat tvam asi"* – "That thou art" (6.8.7), meaning, you are Brahman. Another interpretation is the idea of the same Parabrahman or Ultimate Reality residing in all atmans (or *ātmās*). This means that we are all the children of one Reality.

Another feature of the Upanishadic teachings is to be free from the fear of death. It perceives death of the body as a natural process wherein the atman never dies. The atman is inherently pure, always existing and joyful *(sat, chit* and *ānanda)*.

The principle of karma is another significant teaching of the Upanishads. A person is bound by his karmas, and when he becomes free from them, his atman attains liberation.

The Upanishads contain several instructive stories and dialogues between gurus and disciples that teach about the Ultimate Reality and other metaphysical aspects.

The Katha Upanishad describes the story of Nachiketā, a precocious child. He wanted to know the secret of eternal life from Yama, the lord of death. Despite Yama's offerings of riches and material joys, Nachiketā remained undeterred in his desire to know the secret of eternal life. Finally, Yama imparts to him the immortal knowledge.

In the Chāndogya Upanishad one finds stories that explain the nature of Ultimate Reality and the *guru-shishya* relationship. One such story describes Satyakāma Jābāla's earnest aspiration to attain *brahmavidyā* (divine knowledge). His unquestioning obedience to the guru's word by tending to cows earns him his grace and subsequently *brahmavidyā*.

Another story from the Chāndogya Upanishad describes guru Dhaumya, who commanded his disciple, Āruni, to stop the water from leaking out of his fields. Āruni lay across the breach and stopped the water from flowing out. The guru was pleased with him and blessed him with *brahmavidyā*.

A third story from the Chāndogya Upanishad is related to Shvetaketu, the son of Āruni. On returning from his guru's ashram after completing his Vedic studies, he was filled with pride. Āruni asked, "Have you attained the knowledge whereby all the unknown becomes known?" Shvetaketu said no. Then his father made him dissolve salt in water and taste it, and said that, like salt Brahman or

Prince Dara Shukoh, son of Shah Jahan, translated some of the Upanishads into Persian

Anquetil Du Perron, a French scholar, published a Latin translation of the Upanishads

God is all pervading. With the dawning of this knowledge Shvetaketu shed his ego.

The Upanishads are replete with many such stories and dialogues that deal with spiritual knowledge.

World interest in the Upanishads was awakened after their translations into other languages. The Mughal Prince Dara Shukoh's[11] (1613-1659 CE) spiritual longing and quest for reality inspired him to study the Upanishads. He translated some of them from Sanskrit into Persian in 1657 CE. The French scholar and traveller, Anquetil du Perron (1773-1805), introduced Hindu philosophy to the West by translating some of the Upanishads. Raja Ram Mohan Roy

---

11. Son of Emperor Shah Jahan.

Raja Ram Mohan Roy, founder of
Brāhmo Samāj, made the first English
translation of some of the Upanishads

Arthur Schopenhauer,
a German philosopher

(1775-1833), a Bengali social activist and founder of the Brahmo Sabhā, which was later renamed as Brāhmo Samāj, made the first English translation. In 1876, Max Müller published a German translation.

The Upanishads have been known as the Himalaya of Indian thought. The German philosopher Arthur Schopenhauer (1788-1860) stated, "In the whole world there is no study so beneficial and so elevating as that of the Upanishads. It has been the solace of my life, it will be the solace of my death."[12]

Paul Deussen (1845-1919 CE), Professor of Philosophy at the Universities of Berlin and Kiel, wrote of the Vedānta,

---

12. *A Cultural History of India,* edited by A.L. Basham. New Delhi: OUP, 2008, p.474.

"And so the Vedānta, is the strongest support of pure morality, is the greatest consolation in the sufferings of life and death."[13]

There are many other great scholars who have appreciated and written copiously about the Vedas, Upanishads and other Hindu Shastras.

SUMMARY

1. The Vedas are the foundational shastras of the Hindus. Hindus believe them to be the oldest sacred texts in the world, revealed by God to the enlightened rishis of India. They are known as the Shruti shastras. Shruti means "that which is heard" or revealed. They include the Vedas (Samhitās), Brāhmanas, Āranyakas and Upanishads.

2. There are four Vedic Samhitās, or collections of mantras or hymns that are commonly referred to as the four Vedas: the Rig Veda, Yajur Veda, Sāma Veda and Atharva Veda. The Rig Veda is the oldest and deals with propitiating the devas (gods of nature) through prayers and rituals.

3. The Samhitās contain hymns for simple rituals. The Brāhmana texts explain the meaning and application

---

13. Deussen, Paul. *The Elements of Metaphysics*. London & New York: Macmillan and Co. 1894, p.337.

of the mantras for performing rites and rituals in *yajnas*. The Āranyakas encompass spiritual contemplation and meditation. They mark a shift from ritualism (*karma-kānda*) in the Brāhmana texts to the realm of philosophical ideas in the Upanishads. Thus, the Āranyakas are the links between the Vedas and the Upanishads. Finally, the Upanishads contain the knowledge of Parabrahman, atman, universe and liberation.

4. Some of the concepts dealt with in the Rig Veda are *ruta* (cosmic order), *satya* (moral order), the seeds of *runa* (obligation), hymns of creation and the Ultimate Person or Purusha.

5. The Upanishads are the end parts or culmination of the Vedas, both chronologically and philosophically, so they are known as the Vedānta. In all, there are over 200 Upanishads, of which thirteen are the most ancient and prominent. They reveal the core of Vedic philosophy and comprise the *jnāna-kānda* of the Vedas.

Veda Vyāsa narrates the Mahābhārata while Shri Ganesha writes

2. DHARMA SHASTRAS, ITIHĀSA AND PURĀNAS

INTRODUCTION

The Vedas or Shruti shastras are the primary sacred texts of the Hindus which command the highest authority. Since they were not authored by man but revealed by God to the enlightened rishis they are self-authoritative, needing no external endorsement or legitimacy. Next in importance are the Smruti shastras. Smruti means "remembrance". The Smruti shastras were written by great seers based on the teachings they remembered from their spiritual masters. The authority of these shastras is derived from the spiritual standing of their authors and their congruence with the Vedas. Yet, since the Smruti shastras are man-made, they are considered secondary to the Shruti shastras.

The Smruti shastras include a large number of heterogeneous works like the Dharma Shastras, the Itihāsa or epics (Rāmāyana and Mahābhārata), and the Purānas.

The source of the Dharma Shastras lies in one of the six Vedāngas (limbs of Veda). Among the Vedāngas, the Kalpasutras deal with the correct performance of rituals.

The Kalpasutras include the Shrautasutras, which focus on the performance of public rituals; the Gruhyasutras, which focus on domestic rites; the Dharmasutras, which explain laws and social ethics; and the Sulvasutras (or Sulba), which outline the geometrical rules of construction for *yajna vedis* or fire-altars, etc. The Dharmasutras, of which the Baudhāyana, Gautama, Vashishtha and Āpastamba are important, are the source of the Dharma Shastras. The Dharma Shastras elaborate upon the Dharmasutras and are of a later age. The Dharmasutras are entirely in prose whereas the Dharma Shastras are in verse.

The Dharma Shastras are typically named after their authors. Thus, the Dharma Shastras written by Manu (according to Paurānic tradition he is the forefather of the human race) is called Manu Smruti, by Sage Yājnavalkya the Yājnavalkya Smruti, and by Sage Nārada the Nārada Smruti. These and many other Dharma Shastras prescribe a moral and social code of conduct for individuals, communities and states that encompass the religious, social, political, economical and legal realms.

Another branch of the Smruti shastras are the Itihāsa, which include the Rāmāyana and the Mahābhārata. They are renowned as the great epics of India. The third type of Smruti shastras are the Purānas, which are an invaluable source of religious and historical literature extolling the avatars of God, devas, creation and dissolution of worlds, and royal dynasties. Because it is said that the meaning and purport of the Veda can be understood with the help of the Itihāsa and Purāna shastras,[1] cultivating a proper understanding

Hindu law is based on the Dharma Shastras

of these shastras is essential for understanding Hinduism.

We shall now deal with the Dharma Shastras, Itihāsa (epics) and Purānas in some detail.

1. DHARMA SHASTRAS

The principle of dharma (morality) and its application in all areas of life is of great importance in Hinduism. Dharma is explained by the Vedas, the Smrutis, and the teachings and conduct of one who is *brahmanishtha* (God-realized) and *shrotriya* (one who knows the true meanings of the sacred texts).

The Dharma Shastras are the primary texts of Hindu

---

1. *"Itihāsapurānābhyām Vedam Samupabrumhayet."* Mahābhārata 1.67.

law and code of conduct. They often start with creation narratives and conclude with advice on how to attain final liberation or *mukti*. Many of the Dharma Shastras or Smrutis, such as Manu Smruti, Yājnavalkya Smruti, Nārada Smruti, Pārāshara Smruti, etc., cover three major topics: (1) *Āchāra,* i.e., code of conduct for all varnas (classes) and ashramas (stages of life); (2) *Vyavahāra,* i.e., social and financial dealings and interactions which involve civil, criminal and religious regulations and (3) *Prāyashchitta,* i.e., atonement for moral lapses. The Smrutis also deal with rules of inheritance, laws of marriage and families, the duties of kings and ministers, worship of God, sacraments from birth till death, *yajna* rituals, and customs and manners to be observed in daily life. The moral law consists of *vidhi* (prescriptions or dos) and *nishedha* (prohibitions or don'ts). The Dharma Shastras contain principles of dharma as a universal and all-encompassing law, which applies to different circumstances.

We shall briefly consider the three main Dharma Shastras, namely, the Manu Smruti, the Yājnavalkya Smruti and the Nārada Smruti.

1. MANU SMRUTI

Manu formulated the Hindu code of conduct (social,

moral and spiritual) from the Shruti shastras in an organized way. He gave the Manu Smruti, which is the earliest and most important of all the Dharma Shastras or moral texts available. It is believed to have taken final shape between 200 BCE and 200 CE. It has twelve chapters and 2,694 *shlokas*

Manu Smruti: The Hindu code of conduct

or verses dealing with *āchāra, vyavahāra,* and *prāyashchitta.* The Manu Smruti describes in detail the duties of the four varnas (classes) and ashramas (stages), the duties of the king, council of ministers and chief justice, civil and criminal law, and other aspects of society. Manu explicitly states that, of the four stages, the householder stage *(gruhasthāshrama)* is the most important to society, because it supports the other three ashramas and also allows the fulfilment of the four goals of life (four *purushārthas*). To understand the Manu Smruti clearly, the commentary by Medhātithi (c. 825-900 CE) is considered to be very useful and important.

Gavin Flood writes, "Schopenhauer's philosophical heir, Friedrich Nietzsche (1844-1900), also admired Hindu ideas

*A manuscript of
Yājnavalkya Smruti*

and referred to the 'Laws of Manu' as a text far superior to the New Testament."[2] Many others have admired the depth of the Hindu shastras.

II. YĀJNAVALKYA SMRUTI

The second of the Smruti shastras is the Yājnavalkya Smruti (finalized between 100 BCE and 300 CE), which has 52 chapters and 1,010 *shlokas*. It deals with the three main aspects of human life: *āchāra, vyavahāra* and *prāyashchitta*. It agrees with Manu Smruti in many aspects and makes clear distinctions between civil and criminal law. In its section on *āchāra* or code of conduct (having 13 chapters), it deals with ceremonies of initiation, duties of the four varnas and ashramas, domestic and social duties and rites of purification and *yajna*. In its section on *vyavahāra* (having 25 chapters) it defines the social rights and duties of the householder. Three hundred and seven verses outline

---

2. Cited by Flood, Gavin, *An Introduction to Hinduism*. New Delhi: Cambridge University Press, Foundation Books, First South Asian Edition, 2004, p.269. From Nietzsche, *The Twilight of the Idols and the Anti Christ*. Harmondsworth: Penguin, 1968, pp. 56-9.

legal procedures and titles of litigation. In its section on *prāyashchitta* or atonement (having 14 chapters), it deals with penalties and means to purge sins. The Yājnavalkya Smruti has an important commentary called the Mitāksharā by Vijnāneshwara (c. 1100 CE). India's current code of

Sage Nārada: The author of Nārada Smruti

Hindu law is mainly based on the Yājnavalkya Smruti and the Mitāksharā. The Mitāksharā was first translated into English in 1810 by the English orientalist Henry Thomas Colebrooke.

III. NĀRADA SMRUTI

The Nārada Smruti deals only with the *vyavahāra* aspect, i.e., social dealings and interactions that involve civil, financial, criminal and religious rules and regulations. It has 21 chapters and 1,028 verses and is believed to have been composed between 100 and 300 CE. It is considered to be an important legal text with reference to ancient criminal laws and court procedures. This text mainly follows the Manu

Smruti but differs in some aspects, particular in the area of juristic principles. It is known for its detailed treatment of ordeals called *'divya'*[3] that were employed in courts of law. Manu mentions two forms of ordeals, Yājnavalkya five, and Nārada states nine ordeals.

IV. CONCLUSION

The Dharma Shastras emphasize the practice of dharma for all Hindus for their material, social, moral and spiritual advancement and happiness. They clearly define the duties of the four varnas and ashramas. They also discuss the very important concept of *runa* or obligation to society, family and one's own self. Manu and many others believed that the systems of the four varnas and ashramas were most appropriate for the development and harmony of both the individual and society. In the case of the four ashramas, the first ashrama dictates the observance of *brahmacharya* (celibacy) and dedication to academic study; the second is *gruhasthāsh-*

---

3. *Divya* generally means divine, but when it is used in the Dharma Shastras it means "that which decides a matter in dispute not determined by human means of proof" in a court of law. The suspect could be subjected to an ordeal when eye witness accounts or circumstantial evidence is not available or is not conclusive. The *divyas* range from two to nine, such as, *visha* (administering poison), *koshapāna* (drinking holy water used for bathing an image of worship), *phāla* (licking a red-hot ploughshare), *tāndula* (swallowing of specially prepared rice grains) and *taptamāsa* (taking out heated gold pieces with one's bare fingers).

rama or the life of a householder, during which one
fulfils one's desires to raise
a family and discharge one's
duty to society; the third is
vānaprasthāshrama, in which
one retires from active life to
focus completely on spiritual
matters; and the last is *san-*
nyastāshrama, in which one
completely renounces the

The Dharma Shastras play an important role in preserving the character, unity and strength of Hindu society

world to fully engage oneself in meditation and other spiritual sadhanas.

A thoughtful study of the Dharma Shastras or Smrutis
shows them to be a source of profound ethical guidance,
inspiration and moral strength. Also, while the Smrutis
have their roots mainly in the Vedas, they have allowed
for necessary adjustments in their codes of conduct in light
of continuing societal changes. Because of this flexibility,
Hinduism remains a flourishing religion with continuing
relevance to the world.

The Dharma Shastras have played a very important role
in preserving the character, unity and strength of society.
They preserve dharma or the basic values of life, emphasize

more so upon duties and responsibilities of people towards society rather than mere individual rights and privileges, and make necessary changes to suit the needs of changing times.

2. ITIHĀSA

The Rāmāyana (the story of Bhagwan Rāma's life) and the Māhābharata (the story of the Pāndavas and Kauravas) are two great epics that constitute the Itihāsa (histories) of ancient India. Through the narration of incidents that took place in ancient days, the Itihasas stress the importance of the four *purushārthas:* dharma (virtue), *artha* (wealth), *kāma* (worldly desires) and *moksha* (liberation). The Mahābhārata is known as the fifth Veda, even though it is classified as a Smruti (text of human authorship) and not a Shruti (revelation) text. All castes had access to the Itihāsa. The Rāmāyana and Mahābhārata were written by two great sage-poets, Vālmiki and Veda Vyāsa, respectively. Both the epics have played, and are still playing, a significant role in enriching and shaping the lives of Hindus and Hindu society. Formerly, the Vedas were accessible to only the learned Brahmins, but the epics, which portray the teachings of Hinduism in simple language, were available to all. They describe the history of the royal dynasties, and

Sage Vālmiki scribes the Rāmāyana

teach moral and spiritual values. The two epics became the sources of poetry, dance, drama, art, architecture and folk songs that have been sung and enacted in all Indian languages for thousands of years.

There are a few regionally and linguistically different versions of the Rāmāyana and Gitā, but the moral implications and ideals in them are not different.

1. RĀMĀYANA

Sage Vālmiki's Rāmāyana is a poetic description of Bhagwan Shri Rāma's life. It is in Sanskrit and is known as the *ādikāvya* – first poem. It contains 24,253 *shlokas* in seven books *(kandas)*: Bālakānda, Ayodhyākānda, Aranyakānda, Kishkindhākānda, Sundarakānda, Yuddhakānda and

Uttarakānda. The language of the Rāmayana is simple, beautiful and vivid. It has become so famous that it has become a source of all later Sanskrit epic poems. Like the Māhabhārata, it is recited and enacted in all languages and regions of India as well as in countries like Indonesia, Thailand, and other places where Hinduism has spread.

The story of Rāma[4] is traditionally older than that of the war between the Pāndavas and Kauravas in the Mahābhārata. The Mahābhārata also contains the story of Rāma in brief. Bhagwan Krishna says in the Bhagavad Gitā that he is Rāma among the wielders of weapons.[5]

Bhagwan Rāma, in the Rāmāyana, is shown as a perfect being, an incarnation of virtue to emulate. He lived, ruled and remained within the bounds of propriety, and hence he is called Maryādā Purushottama. The main characters of the epic include King Dasharatha of Ayodhyā and his three wives and sons: Kaushalyā, Sumitrā and Kaikeyi. Kaushalyā was the mother of Rāma, Sumitrā gave birth to two sons, Lakshmana and Shatrughna, and Kaikeyi gave birth to Bharata. Rāma, the eldest, became the crown prince

---

4. According to *Ancient World – A New Look*, edited by N. Mahalingam, published in Madras, 1981, some important dates from Rāma's life in accordance to astronomical descriptions in the Rāmāyana and Purānās have been calculated, namely, Rāma's birth – 4439 BCE, his exile – 4414 BCE and his coronation – 4400 BCE.

5. *"Rāmaha shastra bhrutām aham."* B.G. 10.31.

*The city of Ayodhyā on the bank of River Sarayu,
where Bhagwan Rāma was born*

of Ayodhyā. The night before Rāma's coronation Kaikeyi demanded of Dasharatha the fulfilment of two wishes he had promised many years earlier. The request came as a shocking surprise for the king. Kaikeyi demanded that Rāma be exiled to the forest for fourteen years, and her son, Bharata, be given the throne instead.

Rāma, his wife, Sitā, and Lakshmana spent their years of exile in the forest, patiently bearing discomforts and trials that came their way. In the final year, Sitā was abducted by the evil Rāvana, the king of Lankā. Then with the help of Sugriva, Jāmbavān, Hanumān and the *vānaras* (monkeys), Rāma killed Rāvana and his army and rescued Sitā. Rāma thus destroyed *adharma* and re-established dharma. Finally,

Rāma and Sitā were crowned as the king and queen of Ayodhyā.

The Vālmiki Rāmayana portrays the glory of Rāma as an ideal man, son, brother, husband and king, possessing virtues of truthfulness, nobility, valour and kindheartedness. Sitā is an ideal of fidelity and devotion. The sacrifice, dedication and allegiance of Lakshmana and Bharata to Rāma are incomparable. Hanumānji's humility, devotion and sacrifice to Rāma are extolled in the Rāmāyana.

The Rāmāyana depicts the picture of an ideal man, family and kingdom (Rāma *rājya*). The emphasis is on virtuous conduct, annihilation of evil *(adharma)* and establishment of righteousness (dharma). It has provided enough ideas and ideals to inspire countless to rise from the human level to divine heights.

In the Rāmacharitamānas, the Hindi version of the Rāmāyana text, Tulasidāsa portrays Rāma as an incarnation of Bhagwan Vishnu. His edition of the Rāmāyana inspires devotion and glory of Rāma as God. The verses *(chopāis)* from the Rāmacharitmānas are very popular and sung with devotion in India and abroad. Notably, it is used as the main text for the Rāmalilā, the famous annual dramatic enactment of Rāma's life in North India.

Out of several other vernacular editions of the Rāmā-

*Murtis of Bhagwan Rāma, Sitā and Hanumān
at Swaminarayan Akshardham, New Delhi*

yana Kamban's Rāmāyana in Tamil, Krittivāsa's Rāmāyana in Bengali, Cherman's 'Rāmāyanam' in Malayalam, Ranganātha's 'Rāmāyanam' in Telugu, Giradhara's 'Rāmacharitra' in Gujarati and Madhav's Rāmāyana in Assamese are popular in their respective states. If the worth of a literary work has to be evaluated by the impact it has had on each succeeding generation, then the Rāmāyana of Vālmiki stands out as supreme in world literature. Its influence and effect on Hindu religion, social values, literature, music, dance, drama, paintings, sculptures, in fact, on so many facets of Indian life, is immense and enduring. It has been said that as long as the mountains stand and rivers flow on this earth, the story of Rāma's divine adventures will remain famous in the world.

II. MAHĀBHĀRATA

There are few other works whose influence on all aspects of life in India has been as profound and perpetual as that of the Mahābhārata. Amidst vast diversities in language, culture and philosophical beliefs, Hindus have been brought together by their shared heritage of the Rāmāyana and the Mahābhārata.

The Mahābhārata is an epic account of the people of greater Bhārata (India) written by Veda Vyāsa. With 18

The Kauravas cheat to win a game of dice against the Pāndavas

books (*parvas*) containing about 100,000 Sanskrit *shlokas*; it is eight times the size of Homer's *Iliad* and *Odyssey* combined. The Mahābhārata is a story of triumph of good over evil or dharma over *adharma*. In it, Veda Vyāsa has brilliantly described all the shades of human nature – good, bad and evil – and Bhagwan Shri Krishna's divine role in protecting and preserving dharma.

The popular epic begins with the two brothers, Dhritarāshtra and Pāndu. The younger brother, Pāndu, was appointed as the king, but due to a curse he retired to the forest and died. Subsequently, the blind Dhritarāshtra became the regent and administrator. Pāndu's five sons were known as the Pāndavas and Dhritarāshtra's one hundred sons were called the Kauravas. The Mahābhārata is centred around a feud between these cousins. Duryodhana, the eldest son of Dhritarāshtra and leader of the Kauravas, schemes with his sly maternal uncle, Shakuni, to deceptively win the kingdom of the Pāndavas in a game of dice. Yudhishthira, the eldest of the Pāndavas, loses the game and his kingdom, and he and his brothers are exiled to the forest for thirteen years. After returning, Duryodhana refuses to return their share of the kingdom. Subsequently, a devastating 18-day war follows, leading to the defeat and death of the Kauravas, including that of Duryodhana, Bhishma, Dronāchārya, Karna and many other great warriors. Yudhishthira becomes the king of Hastināpura.

From a mundane perspective, the Mahābhārata was a fierce conflict between cousins. From an ethical standpoint, it was a war between good and evil, justice and injustice; in which the two sides pitted against one another are considered to be analogous to the devas and demons. The war concluded with the victory of dharma. From a metaphorical perspective, the war was not only fought on the grounds of the Kurukshetra, but it is still being fought in our own minds today. It is a battle between the higher and the lower self in man. The Pāndavas, with the help of Bhagwan Shri Krishna (Super-Self), emerged victorious in

*Bhagwan Krishna reveals his divine cosmic form
to Arjuna on the battlefield*

the conflict against the lower self in man in the form of the
Kauravas. The events and teachings of love, war, morality
and sacrifice convey powerful moral, social, political and
spiritual lessons to one and all and for all times to come.

The Mahābhārata reflects the fundamental lesson of what
one can attain through faith and refuge in God. Against
great odds, the Pāndavas were victorious because of Shri
Krishna's grace and divine intervention. It also conveys the
message of *"Yato dharmastato Krushno, yataha Krushnastato
jayaha"* – "Where there is dharma there is Krishna, and
where there is Krishna there is victory."[6]

The essence of the Mahābhārata lies in the Shrimad

---

6. Mahābhārata, Bhishma Parva, 43.60 and Shalya Parva, 62.32.

53

Bhagavad Gitā. The Gitā is a part of the Bhishma Parva of the Mahābhārata and contains the teachings of Shri Krishna to Arjuna on the battlefield. It is a perennial source of social, moral and spiritual inspiration for mankind. The essence of the Shrimad Bhagavad Gitā lies in its last *shloka, "Yatra Yogeshwarah Krushno..."* – "Where there is Krishna and Arjuna (God and his ideal devotee) there certainly will be wealth, victory, power and morality."

The Mahābhārata is more than just a history or *itihāsa* narrated as a poem. It is considered to be an authoritative Dharma Shastra – an encyclopaedia of law, morality, social and political philosophy, that lays down principles for the attainment of dharma, *artha, kāma* and *moksha.* It embraces every aspect of life. Hence it is popularly believed, "Whatever there is in the Mahābhārata one will find elsewhere; and what is not in it cannot be found anywhere else".[7] The fact that many Hindus revere the Mahābhārata as the "fifth Veda" is a testament to its vast scope, profound wisdom and spiritual authority.

The Mahābhārata describes many men and women who shine as beacons of ideal moral conduct and spirituality for humanity. The actions of its heroes have been sung uninterruptedly for centuries by sages, political thinkers,

---

7. Mahābhārata, Swargārohana Parva, 5.50.

poets, dramatists and devotees around the world.
Bhagwan Krishna and Arju-
na are worshipped as Nārāyana and Nara. Their sacred
images, known as Nara-
Nārāyana, are installed in
many mandirs throughout
India.

The Bhagavad Gitā

India's glorious culture
and civilization have survived and progressed partly because
of its shastras, mandirs, divine incarnations, sages, festivals,
social customs and leaders. For centuries, the ideals of the
Rāmāyana and Mahābhārata have been the soul of India's
people, sustaining them in painful and challenging times.

III. BHAGAVAD GĪTĀ

Authored by Veda Vyāsa, the Bhagavad Gitā is a part of
the Bhishma Parva (chapters 25 to 42) of the Mahābhārata, containing 700 *shlokas* in 18 chapters. The Bhagavad
Gitā is believed to be the essence of the Upanishads.

"Sarvopanishado gāvo dogdhā gopālanandanaha,
Pārtho Vatsaha sudhir bhoktā dugdhām gitāmrutam mahat."[8]

---

8. Bhagavad Gitā (Gita Māhātmya: 6).

Shri Gitā Mandir, Ahmedabad

Murti of Shri Gitā Devi, Ahmedabad

"All the Upanishads are like cows, Shri Krishna is the cowherd and Arjuna is the calf, the wise person is the drinker, and the nectar-like milk is the Gitā itself." The Gitā mainly contains the dialogue between Bhagwan Shri Krishna and Arjuna on the battlefield of Kurukshetra more than 5,000 years ago.

The Gitā is one of the three principal texts of Indian philosophy known as Prasthānatrayi. The other two are the Upanishads and the Brahmasutras.

The Bhagavad Gitā, literally means "divine song", was born out of the *vishāda* (sadness) of Arjuna. The battle of the Mahābhārata was about to commence when Arjuna told Bhagwan Krishna, his charioteer, to take his chariot in front of the Kaurava army. On seeing his gurus, elders,

56

kith and kin on the battlefield, Arjuna suddenly became sad and distressed and dropped his bow. He felt it would be impossible for him to kill those to whom he was so attached.

Shri Krishna urged him to fight because it was his duty as a Kshatriya (warrior). He then elaborated upon the fleeting attributes of the body and the eternality of the soul.

The Gitā encompasses religion, ethics, metaphysics and the ideal way of living. The enquiries and doubts posed by Arjuna and the solutions given by Shri Krishna are valid even today. A reading of the holy text confers great religious merit, guidance and inspiration in life. The main teachings in the Gitā are: (a) Yoga, (b) Doctrine of Avatar, (c) Cosmic form of God, (d) Doctrines of Karma and Rebirth and (e) *Guru-shishya* Relationship. We shall now deal briefly with each of them.

A. Yoga

The Gitā has shown three main ways to realize God, namely, Jnāna Yoga, Karma Yoga and Bhakti Yoga.

❖ **Jnāna Yoga (Chapters 1-6):** The path of spiritual wisdom is called Jnāna Yoga. Knowledge or *jnāna* means discrimination between the real and the unreal. It also means realization of one's soul to be imperishable and

Bhakti Yoga:
Offering food to an image of God

immortal, and the body to be perishable and mortal. Shri Krishna explains this immortality of the atman by saying that it cannot be slain, burnt or destroyed in any manner. It is the body which is destroyed and not the atman. One who is born dies and one who dies is born again.[9] Jnāna Yoga also encourages the realization that God resides in all atmans,[10] and therefore every individual possesses divine consciousness.

To attain God-consciousness one needs to discipline the senses, perform spiritual practices and have firm faith. The Gitā praises the *jnāni* or, one who has realized Jnāna Yoga, as being dearest to God.

❖ **Karma Yoga (Chapters 7-12):** The path of action is known as Karma Yoga, where ideally all activities are to be performed without any attachment and expectation (*nishkāma* karma) for their fruits or results. The Gitā does not preach the renunciation of action but renunciation of

9. B.G. 2.27.
10. B.G. 18.61.

the fruit of action.

❖ **Bhakti Yoga (Chapters 13-18):** Having profound love for God is Bhakti Yoga. It is total surrender to God through absolute devotion.

B. Doctrine of Avatar

The Gitā states that God is born on earth in human form to eradicate *adharma* and establish dharma, i.e., to destroy evil elements and protect the pious. In this way, God is the sustainer of the moral order.[11]

C. The Cosmic Form of God

In the eleventh chapter of the Gitā, Arjuna requests Shri Krishna to reveal his cosmic form (Vishwarupa). The Lord blesses Arjuna with divine sight and he sees the effulgent, infinite and awe-inspiring form of Shri Krishna. His Vishwarupa form has infinite arms, and countless faces radiant with the light of innumerable suns and universes. Arjuna also sees the Kaurava army, including Dhritarāshtra, Bhishma, Drona, Karna and its chief warriors being consumed as they enter into the mouth of Shri Krishna's cosmic form. Arjuna is overwhelmed by the immensity of this divine vision, and thus prays to

---

11. B.G. 4. 7-8.

Shri Krishna to revert to his original, serene and beautiful human form. For Arjuna, this incident revealed Shri Krishna's divinity.

D. Doctrines of Karma and Rebirth

The Gītā explains that every karma or action produces a corresponding result. The good and bad karmas are rewarded or punished by God with good or bad fruits. One's karmas are responsible for birth and rebirth, and hence, they are the root cause of suffering. To be liberated from the effects of suffering from karma and rebirth, one has to perform *nishkāma* karma – actions with no desire for their fruits.[12]

E. Guru-shishya Relationship

The Gītā exemplifies a key aspect of the *guru-shishya* relationship,[13] where Bhagwan Krishna, the teacher, imparts knowledge to Arjuna, the disciple. He teaches Arjuna that true knowledge can be obtained by surrendering *(pranipāta)* to the guru, by questioning and asking for clarification of principles *(pariprashna)* and through dedicated service *(sevā)*.[14]

---

12. B.G. 2.51; 3.19; 5.20-21.
13. B.G. 2.7.
14. B.G. 4.34.

Guru imparts spiritual knowledge to his disciples

The message of the Gitā is universal. Its aim is to remedy the conflicts that arise from misidentification with the body *(dehabhāva)*, inordinate attachment to kith and kin *(moha)* and base instincts *(vāsanā*: lust, anger and greed) through absolute refuge in God and selfless performance of one's own karmas.

3. PURĀNAS

The Vedas are the foundational sacred texts of Hinduism. But the language and content of the Vedas were difficult for the common people to grasp. To present its wisdom in an easily understandable manner to the masses, Veda Vyāsa wrote the Purānas, which are a valuable source of ancient religious and historical literature. The Purānas help one

Gurukula students listen to stories from the Purānas

understand and interpret the Vedas. Its language is simpler and the principles and concepts are explained in a more understandable manner. Thus, the Purānas effectively address the religious, social and moral needs of man.

We are indebted to the Purānas for providing us with the Hindu religious practices like meditating on God, *murti-pujā*, *shrāddha* (rites to propitiate one's ancestors), and duties of varnas and ashramas which embrace the sacred and social aspects of human life. Furthermore, they explain the importance and necessity of building mandirs, consecrating the sacred *murtis* of God, and performing daily rituals. They also emphasize the merits of *tapas (austerity)*, *tirtha-yātra* (pilgrimage), *dāna* (donations), and the need for celebration of festivals and many other aspects of daily life and relations.

The Purānas consist of 18 Mahāpurānas ('great Purānas') and 18 Upapurānas ('secondary Purānas'). They deal predominantly with the glory of avatars of God, devas, creation *(sarga)*, dissolution and re-creation *(pratisarga)* of

The devout read, listen to and revere the Purānas

the universe, dynasties of devas *(vamsha)*, the eras of the
14 Manus *(manavantaras)* and the histories of the Solar and
Lunar dynasties of kings *(vamshānucharitra)*.[15]

The 18 Mahāpurānas are: (1) Brahma (2) Padma (3)
Vishnu (4) Shiva (5) Bhāgavata (6) Nārada (7) Mārkandeya
(8) Agni (9) Bhavishya (10) Brahmavaivarta (11) Linga
(12) Varāha (13) Skanda (14) Vāmana (15) Kurma (16)
Matsya (17) Garuda and (18) Brahmānda. Traditionally,
they are divided into three groups of six, out of which one
group focuses upon Bhagwan Vishnu, another on Bhagwan
Brahmā and the third on Bhagwan Shiva. The six Vaishnava
Purānas are the Vishnu, Nārada, Bhāgavata, Garuda,
Padma, and Varāha Purānas. The six Purānas related to

---

15. Swami Harshananda, *A Concise Encylopaedia of Hinduism, Vol. 2.* Bangalore:
Ramakrishna Math, 2008, p.571.

Brahmā are the Brahma, Brahmānda, Brahmavaivarta, Mārkandeya, Bhavishya and Vāmana Purānas. And the six Shaiva Purānas are the Matsya, Kurma, Linga, Shiva, Skanda and Agni Purānas.

Among all the Mahāpurānas, the Shrimad Bhāgavata is the most popular and widely expounded by religious gurus and proponents of the Bhakti tradition. It has about 18,000 *shlokas*, referring to the ten avatars of Bhagwan Vishnu and emphasizing Bhagwan Krishna's life and work. The Bhāgavata Purāna gives importance to bhakti towards God, which is reflected through austerity, charity, tolerance and faith in the lives of devotees like Dhruva, Prahlāda, Harishchandra, Bali, Sudāma, the Gopis and others. The Mārkandeya Purāna is the smallest of all the Purānas, having 9,000 *shlokas*, and the Skanda Purāna is the largest, having 81,000 *shlokas*. A very important work called the Vāsudeva Māhātmya is a part of the Vishnu *khand* (section) of the Skanda Purāna. It emphasizes *ekantika dharma,* i.e., dharma, *jnāna, vairagya* and bhakti, as well as ahimsa or nonviolence.

The growth of the Purāna literature continued through time. They were accommodated under the title 'Upapurānas'. They were considered to be of lesser importance than the Mahāpurānas. Some of the Upapurānas are, Ādi, Narasimha, Kāpila, Kalikā, Vāruna, Vishnudharmottara and Devibhāgavata. The general content of the Upapurānas is on similar lines to the Mahāpurānas. There are also a large number of Sthalapurānas that deal with holy places.

SUMMARY

1. After the Vedas and Upanishads the next authoritative texts are the Smruti shastras which include the Dharma Shastras, Itihāsa, Purānas, Sutra works and others. Smruti means "that which is remembered".

2. The Dharma Shastras were written by Manu, Yājnavalkya, Shankha-Likhita, Parāshara, Nārada and others. They prescribe a moral code of conduct for individuals, communities and states. They deal with the religious, social, political, economical and legal realms of society. The Smrutis are man-made and they have interpreted Vedic principles to guide human practices in changing contexts. Consequently, their canons have grown and some aspects have been changed. This capacity for change has been important for combating the rigidity in traditions and practices that might develop through time and human failings.

3. The Itihāsa comprise the two great epics: the Rāmāyana and the Mahābhārata. Sage Vālmiki wrote the original Rāmāyana. It is a poetic narration of Bhagwan Rāma's life and work. The Rāmāyana portrays the character of an ideal man, family, society and state.

4. The Mahābhārata, written by Veda Vyāsa, is regarded as the fifth Veda by the Hindus. It vividly depicts an epic war between good and evil, justice and injustice, and dharma and *adharma*. In the end, dharma prevails.

5. The Bhagavad Gitā, a part of the Mahābhārata, is the divine discourse of Bhagwan Krishna to Arjuna on the battlefield of Kurukshetra. Bhagwan Krishna urges Arjuna to perform his duty as a Kshatriya, that is, to fight and protect the righteous and punish the wicked. He imparts *jnāna* yoga, karma yoga and bhakti yoga to Arjuna. Eventually, Arjuna rises, fights and wins.

6. The 18 Mahāpurānas and Upapurānas were written by Veda Vyāsa. Through stories, that describe the genealogies of devas and kings, and teachings, they sing the glory of God's avatars, convey theism, devotion to God, philosophy, *murti-pujā*, ethics, festivals, rituals

and ceremonies. They also include cosmology, law codes, moral life, pilgrimages, sacrifices, etc. They are very important literary sources for India's history up to the Gupta dynasty (320 to 600 CE).

The Āgama sacred texts deal with mode of worship, building of mandirs, etc.

3. ĀGAMAS, VEDIC LITERATURE AND VEDIC SCIENCES

INTRODUCTION

The Āgamas, Vedic literature and sciences, Upavedas and Sutra literature form an important part of the corpus of Hindu shastras.

The Āgamas are a class of Hindu religious literature which practically form the basis of almost all Hindu religious practices of the post Vedic era. The name Āgama means "that which teaches the Truth from all aspects", and so its followers hold the Āgamas in equal importance to the Vedas or any sacred book. In practice, they deal with deities like Shiva, Shakti and Vishnu, and also their respective mandirs and worship rituals. The three groups of Āgamas are Shaiva Āgamas, Shākta Āgamas and Vaishnava Āgamas. They deal mainly with philosophical subjects, yogic practices, mandir architecture, science of *murti* consecration, rituals and code of conduct. The Āgamas are treated by their respective followers as equal in importance to the Vedas.

The Vedic literature and sciences include the Vedāngas or "limbs of the Veda", Upavedas ('lesser' or 'complementary'

Vedas) and Sutra literature (short formulaic statements). The Vedāngas are texts of the subsidiary sciences of phonetics, prosody, grammar, etymology, astronomy, geometry and sacrificial rituals that help one understand and study the Vedas in their proper context.

The four Upavedas include Ayurveda (science of medicine), Gāndharvaveda (science of music and dance), Dhanurveda (science of archery and warfare) and Sthāpatyaveda (science of architecture). Some scholars also include Arthaveda or Arthashāstra within the Upavedas.

The Sutra literature consists of short formulaic statements or aphorisms, expressing a general truth. They had to be memorized by students and commented upon and explained by teachers. It includes the Kalpasutras, *Bhaktisutras,* Brahmasutras, *Sānkhyasutras.*

We will examine in detail each of these types of literary forms, beginning with the Āgamas.

1. THE ĀGAMAS

The Āgamas or Tantras[1], like the Vedas (also called

---

1. "The Tantras proper are the Word of Shiva and Shakti." Sir John Woodroffe (1865-1936 CE), a British Orientalist, *Shakti and Shakta, Essays and Addresses on the Shakta Tantrashastra.* London: Luzac & Co., 1918, p. 21.

   "Gradually, it [Tantras] got restricted to a particular class of literature, a literature primarily devoted to the cult of Shakti or the Divine Mother." Swami Harshananda. *A Concise Encyclopaedia of Hinduism, Vol. 3,* 2008, p. 379.

Nigamas), are another class of very sacred Hindu texts. The Āgamas deal with beliefs and practices related to Vishnu, Shiva and Shakti. It is difficult to fix their time of origin, however it can be stated that some of the Āgamas of the early Vishnu sects were in existence by the time of the Mahābhārata. The development of the Āgamas of other schools might have continued till 800 CE.

The Āgamas are considered to be revealed *(shruti)* like the Vedas and are thus held in equal importance and authority by their devout followers.[2] They deal with God, sacred living, mode of worship, building of mandirs, consecration of images, yoga, creation and philosophy.

The three main groups of Hindu Āgamas or Tantras are: Vaishnava, Shaiva and Shākta. There are also the Buddhist and Jain Āgamas or Tantras. Of the Hindu Āgamas, there are 108 main Vaishnava Āgamas, 92 main Shaiva Āgamas and 77 main Shākta Āgamas. Though each of the three groups has different doctrines and regards itself as superior, they share common elements in prescribed spiritual practice (sadhana) and ritual practice. The Āgamas consist of four parts called *pādas*, each having many Sanskrit verses in metrical form: (1) the contents of the *charyā pāda* deal with observance of religious injunctions, right conduct, the *guru-shishya*

---

2. For details see the *Agampramānya* by Yāmunāchārya. Baroda: Oriental Research Institute.

relationship, community life and town planning – with focus on the mandir as its centre, (2) the *kriyā pāda* describes and defines worship rituals and mandir – from site selection for construction of mandir, architectural design, construction methods, iconography (*murti* sculpture), rules for pujaris, festivals and home-shrine rituals; (3) the *yoga pāda* reveals meditation and yogic discipline to purify body and mind and awaken the *kundalini shakti* and (4) the *jnāna pāda* elaborates on philosophical topics like the doctrine and nature of Bhagwan, *jivas, māyā* and the means to attain *moksha*.

A brief description of the three groups of Āgamas follows:

1. Vaishnava Āgamas

The Vaishnava Āgamas, also called Samhitās, consist of the Pāncharātra Āgamas and the Vaikhānasa Āgamas. Both teach that Vishnu is the "Supreme Truth" and the highest deity, and emphasize the various types of worship in mandirs. This worship involves *murtis* of several deities and devotees known as *nitya muktas*.

The Pāncharātra Āgamas were revealed by Bhagwan Nārāyana to five disciples in five nights. They consider Bhagwan Vishnu and Lakshmiji as the principal deities or divine couple *(divya dampati)* and deal extensively with rituals of *murti-pujā*, rules of mandir architecture, and the path of bhakti.

The Pāncharātra Āgamas also prescribe a devotional way of life for followers that include five fundamental practices: (1) going to the mandir and concentrating on God with mind, body and speech *(abhigama)*; (2) collecting materials for the worship of God *(upādāna)*; (3) actual worshipping God *(ijyā)*; (4) studying shastras *(swādhyāya)* and (5) meditating on the *murti* of God (yoga).

Bhagwan Vishnu and Lakshmiji are the principal deities in the Pāncharātra Āgamas

The Vaikhānasa Āgamas claims to have their roots in the Vedas. They deal with daily rituals of making Vedic offerings into fire and the daily worship of Bhagwan Vishnu's *murti* in the inner sanctum of a mandir. The daily worship rituals include welcoming Bhagwan Vishnu as a royal guest and offering him food with the chanting of Vedic mantras. The votaries of Vaikhānasa came to function as chief pujaris in many south Indian mandirs. Even today this is true, particularly at the Tirupati Venkateshwara (Bālāji) Mandir, the most famous Vaishnava pilgrimage centre in Andhra Pradesh, South India.

The Vaikhānasa sect clearly insists upon its purely orthodox or Vedic status.

The *Catalogue of Pāncha rātra,*[3] with about 460 Vaishnava Āgamas, was recently researched and compiled by two BAPS Swaminarayan saint-scholars.

ii. Shaiva Āgamas

The Shaiva Āgamas are the sacred texts of the Shaiva Sampradāya in which Bhagwan Shiva is the presiding deity. They contain information on the Shaiva philosophical doctrine, rituals, worship, religious practices, architecture of Shiva mandirs, sculpture of the *murtis* and art in general. The Shaiva Āgamas say that souls are in bondage, and *moksha* is attained through an understanding of the nature of six principles: (1) Lord (Pati); (2) knowledge *(vidyā)*; (3) false knowledge *(avidyā)*; (4) individual soul *(pashu)*; (5) noose of impurities *(pāsha)* and (6) worship of Shiva *(moksha-kārana)*. They emphasize on the worship of Shiva (Pati) for removing the noose of impurities *(pāsha)* from the individual soul *(pashu)*. Only through Shiva's grace do the souls *(pashus)* attain liberation.

The Shaiva Āgamas principally prescribe *murti-pujā* and rituals, and propagate the realization of Shiva as the ultimate goal.

---

3. *Catalogue of Pāncharātra.* Researched and compiled by Sadhu Shrutiprakashdas and Sadhu Parampurushdas. Gandhinagar, Gujarat: AARSH (Akshardham), 2002.

*Bhagwan Shiva is praised
in the Shaiva Āgamas*

*Durgā is one of the devis praised
in the Shākta Āgamas*

III. Shākta Āgamas

In the Shaiva Āgamas one finds dialogues between
Bhagwan Shiva and Pārvati, in which the former is the
master and the latter his disciple. However in the Shākta
Āgamas, also known as Tantras, the opposite can be seen,
where Pārvati (also known as Sati, Devi, Umā and Kāli) is
the guru and Bhagwan Shiva is her disciple. So it is Shiva
who asks questions to her and Pārvati answers.

There are two main groups of Shākta Āgamas or Tantras:
the Dakshināchāra Tantras or the "right-hand path", also
known as Samaya or Sāmāyika *marga* and the Vāmāchāra
Tantras or the "left-hand path", also called Kaula. The
Dakshināchāra teaches the worship of the deity Dakshina

Kālikā according to Vedic modes of worship and sadhana for ultimate realization. And the Vāmāchāra promotes the ritual use of "five Ms" (*panchamakāras*), namely, wine (*madya*), fish (*matsya*), meat (*māmsa*), posture (*mudrā*) and extra-marital sexual union (*maithuna*) for spiritual realization. So, the Dakshināchāra teaches spiritual practices that are decent and morally acceptable, whereas the Vāmāchāra advocate the belief that even aberrations can be raised to the level where they become spiritual practice, resulting in the realization of Truth.

The Shākta Āgamas teach about the worship of Shakti or the Universal Mother – the female principle of Shiva – namely, Pārvati and her other forms, such as, Durgā, Ambā, Kāli and others. The objective is to attain material power, prosperity and finally liberation.

2. VEDIC LITERATURE AND SCIENCES

There are other shastras which have their origin in the Vedas and were later developed by different rishis. They are known as Vedic literature and sciences and are classified as Smruti shastras. These texts are, (i) Vedāngas (limbs of Vedas), (ii) Upavedas ('lesser' or 'complementary' Vedas), (iii) Sutras (short formulaic statements or aphorisms) which include the Brahmasutras. A brief description of each is as follows:

Students of a gurukula recite Vedic mantras on the banks of River Gangā

I. VEDĀNGAS

To make the spiritual and ritual concepts of the Vedas easily understandable, the rishis developed the Vedāngas – "limbs of the Vedas". These are subsidiary works of Vedic knowledge that help one to study, understand and practice the teachings of the Vedas. The six Vedāngas are Shikshā (phonetics), Chandas (prosody), Vyākarana (grammar), Nirukta (etymology), Jyotisha (Astronomy, Astrology, Mathematics, and Geometry) and Kalpa (Science of sacrificial rites and rituals).

Shikshā and Chandas are aids for pronouncing and reciting Vedic mantras correctly, Vyākarana and Nirukta are for understanding their meaning, and Jyotisha and Kalpa provide appropriate times and methods for performing the Vedic sacrificial rites and rituals. The origins of these six auxiliary 'sciences' are found in the Vedas. A brief description of each of them follows.

❖ Shikshā

This branch teaches the science of phonetics or pronunciation and recitation of the Vedic mantras. Any deviation in the pronunciation can change the meaning and thus mar the desired effect or purpose for which the mantras are chanted and applied in sacrifices.

Some outstanding examples of Shikshā texts include the *Pāniniya Shikshā* by the great grammarian Sage Pānini and the writings of Sage Bhāradwāja.

❖ Chandas

Chandas is the science of prosody. It deals with versification, or the rules for the metres in which Vedic mantras and poems were composed. There are eleven major and minor metres like, Gāyatri, Anushtup, Ushnik, Trishtup, Jagati, etc. Pingala is the earliest known author of the Chanda shastra written in *sutra* form, which became popularly known as *Pingala* shastra.

According to tradition, before reciting any Vedic mantra the reciter has to pay respect to the respective rishi, *devatā* and *chandas* of the mantra.

Ashtādhyāyi is the renowned text on Sanskrit grammar by Pānini

❖ **Vyākarana**

Vyākarana is the science of grammar, which helps to make language clearer. It is called the 'mouth' of the Vedas. Without it, the Vedas and all other Shruti works would be impossible to understand correctly. The earliest available text on Sanskrit grammar today is the *Ashtādhyāyi* of Pānini (c. 500 BCE). Pānini wrote his work for the understanding of the Vedic and mainly the classical Sanskrit language, and especially for the style of Sanskrit spoken in his day. Though the Vedas were revealed and chanted many millennia before him, a systematic grammar for both Vedic and classical Sanskrit was first given by Pānini. The *Ashtādhyāyi* is considered to be the most basic and standard work in Sanskrit grammar today. It has been recognized as one of the greatest intellectual achievements of all time. Pāṇini, however, mentions several scholars who were grammarians and lexicographers before him.

It is worth noting that some ancient grammarians like Patanjali (200 BCE) and Bhartruhari (between 450 and 500 CE) developed a spiritual philosophy out of grammar. They identified the eternal aspect of sound with Brahman (*shabda* Brahman) of Vedānta by writing the *Mahābhāshya* and *Vākyapadiya* respectively. Vyākarana also includes dictionaries like *Amarakosha, Halāyudhakosha* and others.

❖ Nirukta

There was a Sanskrit work called *Nighantu,* now extinct, which was a dictionary of difficult Vedic words. The work is attributed to Yāska by some scholars, but it is not certain who the real author was. According to Yāska, the difficult words were collected and classified by the descendants of ancient sages.

The *Nirukta* is the oldest Indian treatise on etymology, philology and semantics, also ascribed to Yāska. The work is available today, and it is a commentary on the *Nighantu.* It thus enables one to understand the Vedas. Sage Yāska was the last of the commentators on *Nighantu.* His work on *Nirukta* is the best known work available. It is considered to be the earliest Vedabhāshya or commentary on the Vedas. It consists of three parts: (1) a list of synonyms called *Naighantuka Kānda,* (2) a list of words used only in the Vedas called *Naigama Kānda,* and (3) a list of words relating to deities and rituals known as *Daivata Kānda.* In the *Daivata Kānda, Yāska* gives the etymological explanation of the names of the deities. Finally, *Nirukta* ends with instructions, teachings and eulogies of the Vedic devas.

❖ Jyotisha

Jyotisha is the Vedic science of astrology that includes astronomy, geometry and mathematics. Movements of the sun, moon, planets and constellations are observed and recorded in order to fix suitable days and auspicious times for the commencement and conclusion of sacred rites and *yajnas* for various purposes. The influence of the movement of celestial bodies on human life was also studied (astrology). References to eclipses are found in the Rig Veda.

Two Jyotisha books available from the early Vedic period are *Archajyotisha* of the Rig Veda with 36 verses and *Yajusjyotisha* of the Yajur Veda with 43 verses, and from the later period we have the *Atharvajyotisha* with 162 verses.

Later, the astronomy section of *jyotisha* science was gradually advanced by the works of Āryabhatta I

(476 CE), Varāhamihira (580 CE), Brahmagupta (628 CE), Bhāskarāchārya I (700 CE), Āryabhatta II (c. 950 CE) and Bhāskarāchārya II (1114 CE). These rishi-scientists helped in the development of Hindu astronomy and astrology.

❖ Kalpa

Kalpa is one of the Vedāngas which lays down the rules for the correct performance of rituals, ceremonial and sacrificial acts. Kalpa means *prayoga* or practical method to conduct Vedic sacrifices correctly. We will deal with Kalpa in detail in the Sutra literature section, following the section on Upavedas.

II. UPAVEDAS

In addition to the four Vedas and Upanishads there are four Upavedas or subsidiary Vedas. These deal mainly with 'secular' sciences such as Āyurveda (science of medicine), Gāndharvaveda (science of music and dance), Dhanurveda (science of archery and warfare) and Sthāpatyaveda (science of architecture). Some scholars consider Arthaveda or Arthashāstra instead of Sthāpatyaveda as one of the four Upavedas. The four Upavedas are important because they deal with worldly subjects, namely, man, matter and society. They are considered to be very important for their contribution in

Charaka Samhitā is the principal text of Ayurveda

the development of Indian civilization and culture. We shall deal briefly with each of them.

❖ Ayurveda

Ayurveda is a science that deals with 'knowledge of life' and longevity. The main texts of this life science are *Sushruta Samhitā* and *Charaka Samhitā*. Ayurveda deals with medicine and health. A long and healthy physical and mental life is necessary for a prolonged spiritual practice and experience. The source of this science, according to sage Sushruta (600 BCE), lies in the Atharva Veda which is aptly called Bhaishajya Veda (the Veda of medicine and treatment of diseases). Ayurveda includes methods of diagnoses and treatment for physiological and psychological illness. It deals with embryology, hygiene, anatomy, surgery, etc.

Dominik Wujastyk, a Senior Research Fellow at the world-famous Wellcome Centre for the History of Medicine at the University College of London and the author of *The Roots of Ayurveda*, writes in his article 'The Science of Medicine', "Indian medicine, as a systematic and scholarly tradition, begins historically with the appearance of the great medical encyclopedias of Charaka, Sushruta and Bhela about two thousand years ago. Just as Pānini's famous linguistic study of Sanskrit leaps into the historical record fully formed, like the Buddha from Queen Maya's side, so the medical encyclopedias too emerge with a learned medical tradition in an almost fully articulated form."[4] Obviously from this one can infer that medical science must have developed fully in ancient India before the emergence of the *Sushruta Samhitā* and *Charaka Samhitā*.

According to Ayurveda, the material bodies of human beings are composed of *kalā* (protective layer), *dhātu* (component matter), *mala* (eliminations), three *doshas* (humours), *agni* (digestive fire) and *kriyā* (movement or activity). Among these six the most important is the principle of three constitutional elements called humours in the human body, namely, *vāta* (air), *pitta* (bile) and *kapha* (phlegm). *Vāta* (air in body) includes all phenomena

---

4. *The Blackwell Companion to Hinduism,* edited by Gavin Flood. Oxford: Blackwell Publishing, 2005, p.393.

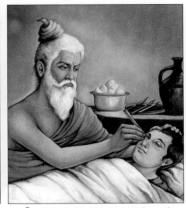

Āchārya Charaka, father of Ayurveda

Āchārya Sushruta, the Father of Indian surgery

of motion and its essential components are ether and air. *Kapha* deals with cooling and preservation, and production of various secretions like mucus and cough. Its essential components are earth and ether. *Pitta* (bile) is made of fire and ether. It deals with metabolism, energy production, process of digestion, etc. A person may be constitutionally brisk (with *vāta* dominating) or fiery (with *pitta* in dominance) or phlegmatic (with *kapha* being the prevalent element). But, according to Ayurveda, only when all three elements are in equilibrium in the human body a person is said to be healthy.

An ayurvedic doctor diagnoses a patient with reference to the relative levels of his or her *vāta, pitta* and *kapha*. The ancient Indian rishis, Charaka and Sushruta, practised

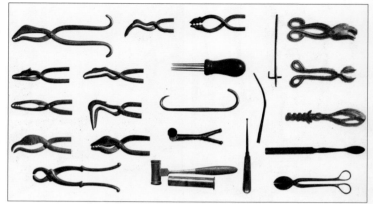

Some of the surgical instruments during Sushruta's time

ayurveda and surgery respectively. Āchārya Charaka (c.100 CE), who wrote the *Charaka Samhitā,* is known as the 'Father of Indian medicine'. Through his intuitive powers he had realized the medicinal qualities of 100,000 plants and herbs. Since the medications are herbal with least side-effects, they are becoming increasingly popular throughout the world.

According to Charaka a long and healthy life is not possible if a person does not live morally. Morality gives rise to *prajñā* or wisdom, which gives peace of mind and leads to longevity and happiness. When this *prajñā* is abused, it causes all types of sickness.

Āchārya Sushruta (600 BCE) is popularly known as the 'Father of Surgery in India'. In the *Sushruta Samhitā,* a unique encyclopaedia of surgery, he details 300 types of operations he performed, along with 125 types of surgical instruments that he used. He is lauded as an early pioneer of plastic surgery and anaesthesia.

Ayurvedic science is divided into eight major topics:

1. Shalya-tantra — surgery and midwifery
2. Shālakya-tantra — study of diseases of head, eyes, nose, throat, etc.
3. Kāyachikitsā — therapeutics
4. Bhutavidyā — mental diseases (psychiatry)
5. Kaumārabhrutya-tantra — paediatrics and obstetrics
6. Agada-tantra toxicology — remedies for venoms
7. Rasāyana-tantra — geriatrics, prevention of disease and improvement of vigour, memory
8. Vājikarana-tantra — prevention of venereal diseases, virilification

Ayurveda also deals with the treatment of plants and animals. Texts of Ayurveda prescribe a strict code of conduct for the physician.

❖ Gāndharvaveda

According to tradition *gandharvas* are expert musicians of *swarga* (the abode of the devas). It is believed that there

Some Indian musical instruments

used to be a work called Gāndharvaveda with 30,000 verses on music, which is not available now.

Gāndharvaveda dealt with the science of music and the sacred performing arts. It derived its origin in the Sāma Veda. It included vocal and instrumental music, dance and drama. There are seven *svaras* (notes) from which *rāgas* are produced, corresponding to the appropriate time of day and season. The *rāgas* create astonishingly powerful physical, psychological and spiritual effects. While Western music has only two modes – major and minor scales – Indian music uses dozens of different modes.

Bharatamuni's *Nātyashāstra,* available today, is an extraordinary text on music, dance and drama.

❖ Dhanurveda

Dhanurveda is the science of archery, martial arts and weaponry. It is a military science, which is mentioned in the Rig Veda and Aitareya Brāhmana. It is also known as *shastravidyā* and it originates from the Yajur Veda. It deals

Tableau depicts ancient Indian weapons,
Swaminarayan Akshardham, New Delhi

with *shastra* and *astra*. *Shastra*[5] means weapons which are used with one's hands in war, such as swords and maces, and *astra* means weapons that are shot like arrows. Dhanurveda also deals with the manufacturing of and training with weapons.

Although there is no ancient scientific work by the name of Dhanurveda, a text called Dhanurveda Samhitā, belonging to a later period, is still extant.

❖ Sthāpatyaveda or Vāstushāstra

Some scholars consider Sthāpatyaveda or Vāstushāstra

---

5. *Shastra* (means weapons) should not be confused with shastra (not italicized because it appears in Concise Oxford English Dictionary, Eleventh edition, 2004.) which means Hindu sacred text.

Vishvakarmā, the divine architect

as one of the Upavedas. It deals with the Hindu science of sacred architecture and the *sthapati* or architect. Traditionally, there are 18 teachers of architecture to whom Sthāptyaveda is ascribed. The two most well known among them are Vishvakarmā (the architect of the devas) and Maya (the architect of the asuras). This important science has its origin in the Yajur Veda, wherein the sacrificial altar or *yajna vedi* was constructed with utmost precision and care in different geometrical patterns. Similarly, Hindu mandirs were built in different styles like Nāgara, Drāvida and Vesara with painstaking perfection by the master builders-cum-architects. It is remarkable that thousands of mandirs of ancient India, in locations as varied as mountains, caves and seashores, still stand today as majestic reminders of this ancient science.

The continuing discovery of various sites of the Indus Valley civilization in the 20th and 21st century conclusively proves that India of remote antiquity had great architects and town planners.

Some of the ancient books on architecture include *Abhilashitārthachintāmani*, *Brihatsamhitā*, *Mānasāra*, *Sama-rānganasutradhāra*, and *Mayamatashilpashāstra*. The *Arthashāstra* of Kautilya and some Purānas, like the Agni Purāna, Matsya Purāna and Padma Purāna, also contain much information about architecture.

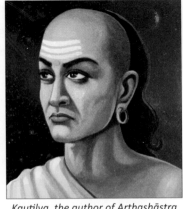

Kautilya, the author of Arthashāstra

❖ **Arthaveda or Arthashāstra**

In ancient India, Arthaveda meant the book containing knowledge of material wealth and the means of acquiring it. The best available work of Arthaveda is the *Arthashāstra* of Kautilya (c. 372 BCE). Kautilya was also known as Chānakya and Vishnugupta. He was the main adviser to King Chandragupta Maurya (340 BCE). Kautilya's *Arthashāstra* has its roots in the Atharva Veda. Shaunaka rishi, in his work *Charanavyuha*, lists *Arthashāstra* as an Upaveda. This work has 6,000 *shlokas* that deal with 180 different topics like politics, law and economics. It is one of the most ancient and brilliant works in the world. In addition to economics it also covers such subjects as relations with enemy states, preparation of army for all types of combat, espionage system, revenue collection, formation of the judiciary and discharging of justice.

III. SUTRA LITERATURE

The Sutra literature is a part of ancient Sanskrit literature, having a unique style of expressing an idea, concept or view in brief through very short statements, formulas or aphorisms. They were introduced because memorizing the increasingly voluminous Smruti literature became impossible. The *sutras* were required in order to carry on the oral tradition, and there are thus a large number of different Sutra works on nearly every traditional subject. Much as a thread in a garland binds everything together, a *sutra*, which literally means 'thread', binds together all aspects of the topics in each work. The *sutras* succinctly deal with the essential ideas or concepts of subjects like religion, philosophy, grammar, and law.

Nearly all systems of Indian philosophy and all subjects of traditional learning in ancient India have their own *sutra* works. In the realm of religion there are Kalpasutras (which has four sections) like the *Bhaktisutras* of Nārada and Shāndilya. In philosophy there are the Brahmasutras (also known as Vyāsasutras or Vedāntasutras), *Mimānsāsutras, Sānkhyasutras, Yogasutras, Nyāyasutras* and *Vaishe-*

The Shrautasutras prescribe the way to perform Vedic yajnas

shikasutras. Pānini wrote the *Ashtādhāyi*, a work of Sanskrit grammar, in the *sutra* style.

❖ Kalpasutras of Kalpa

Kalpasutras deal with social and religious ceremonies and rituals. The Kalpasutras belong to a period later than that of the major ancient thirteen Upanishads. They are divided into four sections:

1. The Shrautasutras are concerned with correct performance of Vedic *yajnas* in public. In them, 'social and spiritual' ceremonies and rituals are described. The authors of the Shrautasutras are Āshwalāyana, Shānkhāyana and others.

2. The Ghruhyasutras give an exposition of domestic ceremonies and rituals related to householders, such as

the sixteen samskaras, duties of teachers, pupils, kings and others. They were also employed for home building, cattle breeding and other activities. The Gruhyasutras of Bodhāyana and Āpastamba are well known.

3. The Dharmasutras explain law, religion, customs, usage and duties of varna and ashrama in life. The well known Dharmasutras are of Sage Gautama and Bodhāyana.

4. The Sulvasutras or Sulbasutras are concerned with rules for measuring and building fire altars for *yajnas*. They were concerned with a subject called *lekhā ganita* – the mathematics of measurement. Their preoccupation with this subject yielded extensive knowledge of elementary geometry. Thus the origin of geometry is believed to be in the Sulvasutras.

❖ BRAHMASUTRAS OR VEDĀNTASUTRAS

The Brahmasutras by Bādarāyana or Veda Vyāsa are also known as Vedāntasutras or Vyāsasutras. They are the sacred philosophical book of *sutras* or aphorisms that summarize the teachings of the Upanishads. The Brahmasutras have 550 *sutras* arranged in four parts, dealing with the Ultimate Reality or Brahman, atman, *jagat, māyā* and *mukti* or *moksha*. The *sutras* are very short statements, sometimes consisting of only two or three words. They cannot be

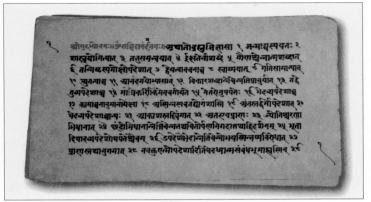

Manuscript of the Brahmasutras

understood properly without a profound teacher of a living tradition or a commentary *(bhāshya)* of the great, erudite *āchārya*.

The Brahmasutras are one of the three most important works of Indian philosophy, called the Prasthānatrayi. The Upanishads are called Shrutiprasthāna, the Brahmasutras are Nyāyaprasthāna and the Bhagavad Gitā is Smrutiprasthāna. *Prasthāna* means a treatise.

The Brahmasutras are a work of philosophy based on logic or Nyāya, whereas the other two are based on Shruti and Smruti traditions respectively. It seems that the Brahmasutras were a part of the ancient oral tradition of the Vedānta system. Their *sutras* were memorized by students and the meanings were explained by authorized teachers.

The Brahmasutras begin with the *sutra, "Athāto Brahma jignāsā",* which means, "Now then [let us have] an enquiry about Brahman," and concludes with the *sutra, "Anāvruttihi sabdāt, Anāvruttihi sabdāt,"* which means, "Not returning back in samsāra, in the mundane world – which means the attainment of *mukti.*"

In the first chapter (or *pāda*) there is a discussion on Brahman as the sole and supreme cause of all things and rejection of other philosophical systems (i.e., Sānkhya, etc.) that do not accept Brahman to be the Supreme Reality.

In the second chapter, arguments for the rejection of Sānkhya continue from the first chapter. The Bhāgavata system is mentioned at the end.

The third chapter deals with *jivātmā.* There is also a discussion on the state of dreams, dreamless sleep, meditation and types of knowledge of Brahman.

The fourth chapter continues discussing the topic of meditation and it ends with the description of conditions of a knower of Brahman after his death.

The Brahmasutras say that Vedic authority is the highest in matters of *moksha.* The Brahmasutras became so popular that almost all the renowned *āchāryas* wrote their commentaries on them. The first commentary available to us is that of Ādi Shankarāchārya who wrote the *Shānkarabhāshya* to establish his own school of Kevalādvaita Vedānta.

Some of the *āchāryas* who have written commentaries on the Brahmasutras are as follows:

	Commentator	Sampradāya or School of Vedānta	Name of Bhāshya on the Brahmasutras
1.	Ādi Shankarāchārya	Kevalādvaita	*Shānkarabhāshya*
2.	Bhāskarāchārya	Bhedābheda	*Brahmasutra bhāshya*
3.	Rāmānujāchārya	Vishishtādvaita	*Shribhāshya*
4.	Nimbārkāchārya	Dvaitādvaita	*Vedāntaparijāta-saurabha*
5.	Madhvāchārya	Dvaita	*Brahmasutra bhāshya*
6.	Vallabhāchārya	Shuddhādvaita	*Anubhāshya*
7.	Baldevāchārya	Achintyabhedābheda	*Govindabhāshya*
8.	Shripati	Dvaitādvaita	*Shrikarabhāshya*

The above mentioned eight well-known schools of Vedānta are but a few of the many important ones. Each of the *āchāryas* explained the most diverse philosophical and theological views in their interpretation of the very same aphorisms. They have the liberty to interpret, because the *sutras* are brief, containing mostly two, three or four Sanskrit words which have more than two or three meanings.

Undoubtedly the Brahmasutras have influenced all important aspects of Hindu philosophy, religion and culture, including the modern Hindu movements.

Six Darshanas		Sānkhya	Yoga	Nyāya	Vaisheshika	Purva Mimānsā	Uttar Mimānsā (Vedāntā)	+	Commentaries of all āchāryas and other related shastras
VEDIC Literature & Sciences		**VEDĀNGAS**			**UPA-VEDAS**				**SUTRAS** - Shrauta - Ghruhya - Dharma - Sulva - Brahmasutras
		Shikshā	Vyākarana	Jyotisha	Āyurveda		Gāndharvaveda		
		Chandas	Nirukta	Kalpa	Dhanurveda	Sthāpatya-veda	Arthaveda		
ĀGAMAS		**VAISHNAVA**		**SHAIVA**			**SHĀKTA**		
		Pāncharātra	Vaikhānasa	Pradhāna		Upa	Vāmāchāra		Dakshināchāra

SMRUTIS	Itihāsa	**RĀMĀYANA** - Vālmiki Rāmāyana - Tulasikruta Rāmāyana (Rāmacharitamānas)				**MAHĀBHĀRATA** - Vidurniti - Moksha-dharma - Bhagavad Gita - Vishnu Sahasranāma			
	Purānas	**SHRIMAD BHĀGAVATA** - Kapila Gita - Rāsa-panchādhāyi - Guna-vibhāga - Vedastuti		Bhavishya Purāna	Vishnu Purāna	Mārkandeya Purāna	Varāha Purāna		
				Nāradiya Purāna	Brahmānda Purāna	Brahma Purāna	Vāmana Purāna		
		SKANDA PURĀNA - Vishnukhand - Vāsudeva Māhātmya		Kurma Purāna	Padma Purāna	Brahma-vaivarta Purāna	Agni Purāna		
				Linga Purāna	Garuda Purāna	Shiva Purāna	Matsya Purāna		
	Dharma Shastras	Manu Smruti	Yājnavalkya Smruti	Parāshara Smruti	Shankha-Likhita Smruti	and Others			

SHRUTIS	Vedas	Upanishad	Upanishad	Upanishad	Upanishad
		Āranyaka	Āranyaka	Āranyaka	Āranyaka
		Brāhmana	Brāhmana	Brāhmana	Brāhmana
		Rig Veda (Samhitā)	Yajur Veda (Samhitā)	Sāma Veda (Samhitā)	Atharva Veda (Samhitā)

SUMMARY OF THE MAIN HINDU SHASTRAS

SUMMARY

1. The Āgamas are believed by some to match the Vedic texts in spiritual and religious authority. They prescribe the mode of worship of deities in mandirs and prescribe a way of life in relation to the systems of devotion and worship.

2. The other shastras include the Vedāngas or limbs of the Vedas and the Upavedas or 'complementary' Vedas. The Vedāngas include Shikshā (phonetics), Chandas (prosody), Vyākarana (grammar), Nirukta (etymology), Jyotisha (astronomy, astrology, mathematics and geometry), and Kalpa (science of sacrificial rites and rituals).

3. The Upavedas or subsidiary Vedas, derived from the Vedas, are Āyurveda (science of health), Gāndharvaveda (science of music), Dhanurveda (military science) and Sthāpatyaveda or Vāstuveda (the science of sacred and 'secular' architecture).

4. The Brahmasutras or the Vedāntasutras are a systematization of the teachings of the ancient Upanishads by Bādarāyana Veda Vyāsa. They are one of the three shastras that form the Prasthānatrayi. The other two are the Upanishads and the Bhagavad Gitā. Almost all the great *āchāryas* have written commentaries on them to establish their own independent Vedānta philosophies.

Bhagwan Swaminarayan delivering a discourse in Gadhadā, Gujarāt

4. THE VACHANĀMRUT
Sacred Text of Spiritual Discourses
by Bhagwan Swaminarayan

The Vachanāmrut is the main religious text of the Swaminarayan Sampradāya. The name means 'words (*vachana*) of immortalizing nectar (*amrut*)'. It contains spiritual discourses delivered by Bhagwan Swaminarayan (1781-1830 CE) in which he has communicated the esoteric truths of the Hindu shastras in a down-to-earth manner. His presentation in the form of dialogues riveted the *paramhansas* and rural devotees in his assemblies. He encouraged them to think, understand and practise spirituality in their daily lives. He candidly reveals, "What I am about to say to you, I state not out of pretence, or out of self-conceit, or to spread my own greatness." Such personal purity and transparency reflect the importance and worth of his discourses.

From 1819 to 1829 CE his discourses were scribed by four of his scholarly *paramhansas*: Muktanand Swami, Gopalanand Swami, Nityanand Swami and Shukanand Swami. They also edited and compiled them into 262 discourses (with 11 more in the addendum) in the lifetime of Bhagwan Swaminarayan and called the collection the

Vachanāmrut. Nityanand Swami presented the Vachanām-rut to Bhagwan Swaminarayan (Vachanāmrut, Loyā 7), who approved of it and blessed the *paramhansas*. It is acclaimed as the first work of modern Gujarāti prose.

The first paragraph of every discourse vividly describes the time, day, date, year, place, and clothes and decorations worn by Maharaj. The Vachanāmruts were delivered at various places of Gujarāt like Gadhadā, Sārangpur, Kāriyāni, Loyā, Panchālā, Vartāl, Ahmedābād, Aslāli and Jetalpur.

In Gadhadā, where Bhagwan Swaminarayan mainly stayed, he spoke seated beneath a neem tree in the *darbār* of Dādā Khāchar. He mostly wore white clothes and, akin to the Upanishadic dialogue tradition, he commenced by discoursing or asking a question or inspiring the audience to voice their questions. The serene, rural ambience of Gadhadā provided a perfect backdrop to the lucid spiritual dialogues. The content of the Vachanāmrut is theological, philosophical and spiritual, dealing with the nature of *jiva, ishwara, māyā*, Brahman and Parabrahman. It also includes the principles of *moksha*, the indispensability of a guru, happiness, misery, non-violence, prayer, bhakti, morals, good company, service, positive attitude, introspection, dhyan and many other practical aspects of daily life

A manuscript of the Vachanāmrut

and spiritual sadhana. Bhagwan Swaminarayan often quoted from the Vedas, Upanishads, Rāmāyana, Mahābhārata, Bhagavad Gitā and Shrimad Bhāgavata during his discourses. At many places he elaborated upon the scriptural references and also gave his own interpretations.

Let us briefly see some examples given by Bhagwan Swaminarayan in the Vachanāmrut about the importance of the Hindu sacred texts.

Belief in Authority of the Sacred Texts

Bhagwan Swaminarayan asked a Vedānti Brahmin about why he propagated the reality of Parabrahman only and ne-

Pramukh Swami Maharaj explains a Vachanāmrut in a satsang assembly

gated the realities of *jiva, ishwara* and *māyā* and the Vedas, Purānas and other shastras. He asked the scholar to reply on the basis of the Vedas, Purānas, Smrutis and the Itihāsa. In addition, Bhagwan Swaminarayan asserted that if the scholar reinforced his argument by quoting Veda Vyāsa then he would accept it, because he had firm faith in the words of Veda Vyāsa (Vachanāmrut, Gadhadā I 39).

The Sacred Texts Sanctioned in the Swaminarayan Sampradāya

The eight authoritative shastras in the Swaminarayan Sarpradaya as endorsed by Bhagwan Swaminarayan are as follows:

1. Vedas

Manuscript of Bhāgavata Purāna

2. Brahmasutras or Vyāsasutras
3. Shrimad Bhāgavata Purāna
4. Vishnusahasranāma from Mahābhārata
5. Bhagavad Gitā
6. Vidurniti
7. Vāsudeva Māhātmya from Skanda Purāna and
8. Yāgnavalkya Smruti (Vartāl 18).

Essence of Sacred Texts

Bhagwan Swaminarayan revealed his principle of serving a God-realized devotee in order to attain God's blessings and pleasure. He corroborates this statement by stating that it is the essence of the words that he has listened to from the Vedas, Purānas, shastras and other such words on earth related to liberating one's soul. He further described the principle of serving a God-realized devotee to be the essence and quintessence of all the shastras (Gadhadā II 28).

Core Principle of All Sacred Texts

Bhagwan Swaminarayan explained the essence of the Vedas, Purānas, Itihāsa and other shastras: till a devotee does not perceives the pleasant and unpleasant worldly objects to be equal he is a *sādhaka* or one who is treading the path of spiritual realization. However, when they (worldly objects) do appear equal, the devotee is said to have attained God realization and he experiences inner fulfilment. He adds that what he has proclaimed is a core principle of all the sacred texts (Gadhadā II 1).

Five Eternal Realities

Taking the scriptural authority of the Vedas, Purānas, Itihāsa and Smruti shastras Bhagwan Swaminarayan stated the principle that *jiva, ishwara, māyā,* Brahman and Parabrahman are all eternal realities (Gadhadā III 11).

God's Form

Bhagwan Swaminarayan clearly stated that the Purānas, Mahābhārata and other shastras say that Bhagwan is the all-doer and that he eternally has a human form (Panchālā 1). The Vedas, Purānas, Mahābhārata, Smrutis and other shastras proclaim that the original form of God is eternal and divine (Panchālā 4).

Murti of Bhagwan Swaminarayan. God has a divine human form

Understanding God's Form Through Four Sacred Texts

Bhagwan Swaminarayan defined that only one who has understood the description of God's form from the Vedas, Sānkhya, Yoga and Pancharātra shastras has attained true knowledge of God's form. One who knows Bhagwan's form through these four shastras is a true *jnāni* (one who has knowledge of God) (Vartāl 2).

Only God and His Sadhu Can Grant Liberation

Bhagwan Swaminarayan said that the four Vedas, the Purānas and the Itihāsa shastras teach the important principle that only God or his realized Sadhu can grant liberation (Gadhadā II 59).

Gateway to Moksha

Bhagwan Swaminarayan emphasized, citing various sacred texts, that a God-realized Sadhu is the means to *moksha*. In this respect he was once asked by his *paramhansa*-disciple about a dialogue between King Janaka and the nine Yogeshwaras (ascetics) in the 11th chapter of the Shrimad Bhāgavata about how to foster Bhāgavata Dharma and the way to attain *moksha*. Bhagwan Swaminarayan replied with a quote from the Shrimad Bhāgavata (3.25.20) that a profound association with the Ekāntika Sadhu, who is wedded to dharma, *jnāna, vairāgya* and bhakti coupled with God's greatness, is the means to nourish Bhāgavata Dharma and attain *moksha* (Gadhadā I 54).

Ekāntika Dharma

Bhagwan Swaminarayan described *ekāntika dharma* as comprising of dharma (righteousness), *jnāna* (spiritual knowledge), *vairāgya* (detachment from sense pleasures) and bhakti (devotion to God). He explained that *ekāntika dharma* was indispensable for attaining *moksha*. In Vachanāmrut Gadhadā II 28 he approves of the Vāsudeva Māhātmya in the Skanda Purāna as an incomparable sacred text, because it firmly propounds dharma, *jnāna, vairāgya* and bhakti (*ekāntika dharma*), as well as ahimsa (non-violence).

The primary purpose of Bhagwan Swaminaryan's mission on earth was to establish *ekāntika dharma* so that souls could attain ultimate liberation.

Overcoming Māyā

Citing the Udyog-parva of the Mahābhārata Bhagwan Swaminarayan empha-

Manuscripts of Ishāvāsya Upanishad and Yāgnavalkya Smruti

sizes to an aspirant that the renunciation of laziness and infatuation for worldly objects is the means of liberation from *māyā* (Sārangpur 14).

How to Attain Spiritual Knowledge and Imbibe Moral Values?

The Vachānamrut explains that spiritual knowledge (*jnāna*) can be acquired through listening to the Brihadāranyaka, Chāndogya, Kathavalli and other Upanishads, Bhagavad Gitā, Vasudeva Māhātmya, Vyāsasutra and other shastras from a God-realized person (Satpurusha). To attain dharma (righteousness) in one's life, one needs to listen (or read) to the Yāgnavalkya Smruti, Manu Smruti, Parāshar Smruti

Sitāji reveals the reason for her grief to Lakshmanji

and Shankh-Likhit Smruti. By doing so one is imbued with dharma and can strengthen one's faith in the shastras (Loyā 9).

Sitāji's Understanding

Elaborating upon the type of devotee who would not find fault in another, Bhagwan Swaminarayan cited from the Rāmāyana, highlighting the faithfulness and allegiance of Sita towards Rāma. He described that when Sitāji was exiled to the forest by Bhagwan Rāma, she broke down on reaching the ashram of Sage Vālmiki. On seeing her grief, Lakshmanji, the brother of Rāma, who had escorted her to the ashram, became very sad. Subsequently, Sitāji revealed that she was not crying at her fate but at Rāma's unhappiness, which stemmed from his awareness that he had wrongfully exiled her.

Sitāji told Lakshmanji to tell Rāma that she was not distressed by her own plight and would happily remember and worship him at Vālmiki's ashram.

Sitāji did not perceive fault in Bhagwan Rāma's action

because of her abiding faith in him (Gadhadā III 11).

In the Vachanāmrut, Bhagwan Swaminarayan discusses scriptural authority, essence of the shastras, the number of eternal realities, God's form, liberation of the soul, *ekāntika dharma*, transcending *māyā*, Sitāji's understanding and many other topics. Regarding the ultimate goal of life he states the outstanding principle of becoming *brahmarup* and offering bhakti to Paramātmā.

The array of spiritual subjects, practical problems and enquiries he deals with in the Vachanāmrut amply show his deep study and profound knowledge of the shastras. They also reflect his faith in the Hindu shastras and his spontaneity in citing scriptural references in his discourses.

There are many other topics, besides those mentioned here, which he had explained, consolidated or solved through references of the Hindu shastras. In some cases he has also given his own unique interpretations. The Vachanāmrut[1] is a distillation of the Hindu sacred texts, explaining the philosophy of Bhagwan Swaminarayan, in a simple and easily understandable form.

---

1. The Vachanāmrut has been translated into English and Hindi.

5. OPINIONS ON HINDU SACRED TEXTS

The Countess of Jersey (1753-1821 CE)

"The doctrines of the Upanishads (the philosophical speculations of the Vedas) satisfy the utmost longings of the mind. The acute logic of the ancient Rishis has raised a bulwork of arguments to support the huge fabric of Hindu thought. The doctrine of Karma offers the simplest and most reasonable answer to the obvious inequalities and striking contrasts in this visible world of happiness and suffering. The ferment and unrest of the soul in the search of knowledge is soothed and laid at rest when the object of contemplation is reduced to a figurehead, and finally a point in space. This contemplation of point in space results in a self-absorbing delight which knows no end, and which places the soul high above all carnal wants and aspirations. This is the goal of Hindu philosophy."[1]

Arthur Schopenhauer (1788-1860 CE)

German philosopher

"In the whole world there is no study so beneficial and so

---

1. Sardar, Har Bilas. *Hindu Superiority,* Ajmer: Rajputana Printing Works, 1906, p. 438.

Arthur Schopenhauer

Ralph Waldo Emerson

elevating as that of the Upanishads. It has been the solace of my life, it will be the solace of my death."[2]

Ralph Waldo Emerson (1803-1882 CE)
American essayist, philosopher and poet

"I owed a magnificent day to the *Bhagavat Geeta*. It was the first of books; it was as if an empire spake to us, nothing small or unworthy, but large, serene, consistent, the voice of an old intelligence which in another age and climate had pondered and thus disposed of the same questions which exercise us."[3]

2. *The Sacred Books of the East.* Edited by F. Max Müller, translated by various Oriental Scholars. Oxford: Clarendon Press, 1879, p. lxi.
3. *Journals of Ralph Waldo Emerson, Vol.7,* edited by Edward Waldo Emerson and Waldo Emerson Forbes. London: Constable & Co. Ltd., and Boston and New York: Houghton Mifflin Company, 1913, p.511.

Henry David Thoreau

Max Müller

Henry David Thoreau (1817-1862 CE)

American author, historian and philosopher

"In the morning I bathe my intellect in the stupendous and cosmogonal philosophy of the Bhagvat Geeta, and in comparison with which our modern world and its literature seem puny and trivial."[4]

Professor Max Müller (1823-1900 CE)

Oxford Sanskrit scholar

"That literature (ancient literature of India) opens to us a chapter in what has been called the Education of the Human Race, to which we can find no parallel anywhere else.

"I maintain that to everybody who cares for himself,

---

4. Thoreau, Henry David. *Walden or, Life in the Woods.* 1854. p.247.

for his ancestors, for his history, or for his intellectual development, a study of Vedic literature is indispensable."[5]

Swami Vivekananda

Paul Deussen (1845-1919 CE)
Prof. of Philosophy at the Universities of Berlin and Kiel

"And so the Vedānta is the strongest support of pure morality, is the greatest consolation in the sufferings of life and death."[6]

Swami Vivekananda (1863-1902 CE)
Torchbearer of Hinduism

"The teachings of Krishna as taught by the Gita are the grandest the world has ever known. He who wrote that wonderful poem was one of those rare souls whose lives sent a wave of regeneration through the world."[7]

---

5. Müller, F. Max. *India What Can It Teach Us?*. London: Longmans, Green, And Co., 1883. pp. 89 & 112.
6. Deussen, Paul. *The Elements of Metaphysics*. London & New York: Macmillan and Co. 1894, p.337.
7. *The Complete Works of Swami Vivekananda*, Vol. 7. Eighth Edition. Calcutta: Advaita Ashrama, 1972, p. 22.

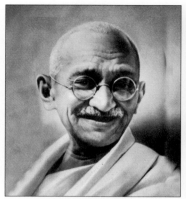

Mahatma Gandhi

Aurobindo Ghosh

Mahatma Gandhi (1869-1948 CE)

Apostle of non-violence

"The Gita, I had read somewhere, gave within the compass of its 700 verses the quintessence of all the shastras and the Upanishads. Today the Gita is my mother. When I am in difficulty or distress, I seek refuge in her."[8]

"When disappointment stares me in the face and all alone I see not one ray of light, I go back to the Bhagavad Gita. I find a verse here and a verse there, and I immediately begin to smile in the midst of overwhelming tragedies — and my life has been full of external tragedies — and if they have left no visible or indelible scar on me, I owe it all to the teaching of Bhagavad Gita."[9]

---

8. Gandhi, M.K. *Harijan,* 24.8.1934, p. 221.
9. *The Vedanta Kesari,* Vol. 95, No. 12, Chennai: Sri Ramakrishna Math, December 2008, p. 161.

Sri Aurobindo
(1872-1950 CE)
Indian mystic and guru

"The Gita is the greatest gospel of spiritual works ever yet given to the race... our chief national heritage, our hope for the future."[10]

Albert Einstein

Dr Albert Schweitzer
(1875-1965)
German theologian, philosopher, physician and medical missionary

"The Bhagavad-Gita has a profound influence on the spirit of mankind by its devotion to God, which is manifested by actions."[11]

Albert Einstein (1879-1955 CE)
Theoretical physicist

"When I read the Bhagavad Gita and reflect about how God created this universe everything else seems so superfluous."[12]

---

10. *The Vedanta Kesari,* Vol. 95, No. 12, Chennai: Sri Ramakrishna Math, December 2008, p. 161.
11. Ibid. p. 162.
12. Ibid. p. 162.

Pandit Jawaharlal Nehru

Aldous Huxley

Pandit Jawaharlal Nehru (1889-1964 CE)

First Prime Minister of India

"The Gita deals essentially with the spiritual background of human existence. It is a call to action to meet the obligations and duties of life, but always keeping in view that spiritual background and the larger purpose of the universe."[13]

Aldous Huxley (1894-1963 CE)

Eminent English writer and philosopher

"The Gita is one of the clearest and most comprehensive summaries of the Perennial Philosophy ever to have been done. Hence its enduring value, not only for Indians,

13. Nehru, Jawaharlal. *Jawaharlal Nehru The Discovery of India.* Delhi: Oxford University Press, 1994. p. 109.

but for all mankind. The Bhagavad Gita is perhaps the most systematic spiritual statement of the Perennial Philosophy."[14]

14. *The Vedanta Kesari,* Vol. 95, No. 12, December 2008, Sri Ramakrishna Math, Chennai, p. 164.

6. FREQUENTLY ASKED QUESTIONS (FAQs)

1. What are the Vedas?

The Vedas are a collection of sacred prayers. The word 'Veda' is derived from the Sanskrit root word 'vid' which means 'to know'. Hence, the Vedas mean knowledge. They were revealed to the ancient rishis by Paramātmā while they were in deep meditation.

2. How many Vedas are there?

There are four Vedas, i.e., Rig Veda, Yajur Veda, Sāma Veda and Atharva Veda. In the broader sense they embrace the Samhitās, Brāhmanas, Āranyakas and Upanishads.

3. What are the Samhitā texts?

The four Samhitā texts are Rig, Yajur, Sāma and Atharva Samhitās. They consist of mantras and verses of prayer to the nature gods for riches, children, long life, peace and eternal happiness. The texts also deal with creation, philosophical ideas, marriage rituals and domestic rites.

4. What are the Brāhmana texts?

The Brāhmana texts are in prose and are known as ceremonial handbooks that deal with the rules and regulations for performance of the various *yajnas* (fire rituals). They contain interesting dialogues, myths and stories, but little philosophy.

5. What are the Āranyaka texts?

The Āranyaka texts discuss the spiritual significance of Vedic *yajnas* and devas. They were the result of contemplation by yogis and rishis in the forests. They marked the transition from ritualism to spiritual contemplation.

6. What are the Upanishads?

The Upanishads contain the core of Vedic philosophy and theology, and chronologically they are the end or concluding part of the Vedas, therefore they are known as Vedānta. The Upanishads describe the glory and attributes of God, and the nature of *jagat* (world) and atman (soul) and their relation to God. According to tradition there are more than 200 Upanishads. Of these ten are the most prominent – Isha, Kena, Katha, Prashna, Mundaka, Māndukya, Taittiriya, Aitareya, Chāndogya and Brihadāranyaka.

Each Upanishad belongs to one of the four Vedas.

7. What are the Smruti Shastras?

The Smruti shastras were written by great seers based on the teachings they remembered from their spiritual masters. These texts were based on the Vedas, and as they are man-made they are considered secondary to the Vedas.

The Smruti texts include the Dharma Shastras, the Itihāsa or epics (Rāmāyana and Mahābhārata) and the Purānas.

Briefly, the Dharma Shastras are *niti* shastras i.e., texts on code of conduct. They deal with social, moral and political laws. They include the Manu Smruti, Yāgnavalkya Smruti, and others.

The Itihāsa are historical accounts of Bhagwan Rāma's life and work (Rāmāyana) and the great war between the forces of good and evil (Mahābhārata).

The Purānas, which form the third category of Smruti literature, are invaluable sources of religious and historical narrations on the avatars of God, devas, cosmic creation and destruction and royal dynasties.

8. What are the Āgamas?

The Āgamas are Hindu religious literature which are the basis of all Hindu religious practices generally of the post-Vedic age. They deal with philosophy, yogic practices, mandir architecture, consecration of *murti*, rituals and code of conduct in relation to the deities of Shaiva, Shakti and Vishnu. The three groups of Āgamas are the Shiva Āgamas, Shākta Āgamas and Vaishnava Āgamas. Their respective followers treat them on par with the Vedas.

9. What are the Vedāngas?

The Vedāngas ('limbs of the Vedas') enable one to study, understand and practise the teachings of the Vedas. They comprise of six branches: 1. Shikshā: The science of pronunciation and recitation of Vedic mantras, 2. Chandas: The rules for the metres in which Vedic mantras are composed, 3. Vyākarana: Sanskrit grammer to enable one to understand the Vedas and other works correctly, 4. Nirukta: A work on the etymology, philology and semantics of Sanskrit language to enable one to understand the Vedas, 5. Jyotisha: The Vedic science of astronomy and astrology. It enables one to perform *yajnas* and sacred rituals on suitable days and at auspicious times, and 6. Kalpa: The rules for correct performance of rituals and ceremonial and sacrificial acts.

10. What are the Upavedas?

The Upavedas are in addition and subsidiary to the four

Vedas. There are four Upavedas: 1. Ayurveda: The traditional life-science that deals with medicine and health, 2. Gāndharvaveda: Encompasses music and the performing arts, like dance and drama, 3. Dhanurveda: The science of archery, martial arts and weaponry, 4. Sthāpatyaveda: The Hindu science of sacred architecture.

11. What is the Sutra Literature?

The Sutra literature comprises of short statements, formulas or aphorisms. The aphorisms summarize the voluminous Smruti and other texts to facilitate oral transmission from one generation to another. They deal with the essential principles of religion, philosophy, grammar and law. All the systems of Indian philosophy have their Sutra works, e.g. Brahmasutras or Vedāntasutras, Yogasutras, Bhaktisutras of Narada, etc.

12. What are the Purānas?

The Vedas are the primary sacred texts of Hinduism. But since they were difficult for the masses to understand Veda Vyāsa wrote the wisdom of the Vedas in a lucid manner in the form of the Purānas. The Purānas are invaluable sources of ancient religious and historical literature. Along with the descriptions of the creation of universes, moral education and the history of kings, they emphasize on the life and works of various avatars and rituals like *murti-puja* (image worship), *shrāddha* (rites to please one's ancestors) and duties of varnas (classes) and ashramas (stages of life).

There are 18 Mahāpurānas ('great Purānas') and 18 Upapurānas ('secondary Purānas'). The Mahāpurānas include Brahma Purāna, Padma Purāna, Vishnu Purāna, Bhāgavata Purāna and others. The Shrimad Bhāgavata Purāna is the most popular of all Purānas and is widely propounded by gurus and savants of the Bhakti tradition.

13. What do the Vedas Contain?

They deal with the glory of deities like Agni (fire-god), Indra (rain-god), Varuna (sea-god) and others. They also deal with creation, *yajna* rituals and secular topics like marriage, wars, statecraft, diseases and cures, architecture, commerce and other things. In brief, they teach both *para vidyā* (spiritual knowledge) and *aparā vidyā* (worldly knowledge).

14. What is the Bhagavad Gitā?

The Bhagavad Gitā is part of the Bhishma Parva of the Mahābhārata, containing 700 *shlokas* in 18 chapters. It literally means 'divine song' and it is mainly the dialogue between Bhagwan Shri Krishna and Arjuna prior to an epic battle. The messages of the Gitā include religion, ethics, metaphysics and the ideal way of living. It is a treatise that deals with yoga, the doctrine of avatar, the cosmic form of God, the principles of karma and rebirth, and the *guru-shishya* relationship.

15. What are the Brahmasutras?

Authored by Veda Vyāsa or Bādarāyana they are also known as the Vedāntasutras or Vyāsasutras. They summarize the teachings of the Upanishads in about 550 aphorisms or *sutras*. They cannot be fully understood without a profound teacher. The Brahmasutras begin with the aphorism, "*Athāto Brahma jignāsā*", which means "Now then [let us have] an enquiry about Brahman." And it ends with "*Anāvruttihi shabdāt, anāvruttihi shabdāt*", which means "Shastra leads to final freedom, Shastra leads to Final Freedom."

16. What is the Prasthānatraya?

The Vedānta system in Hindu philosophy is based on the Prasthānatraya – the three principle works that enable one to realize the final goal of life. They are the Upanishads, Bhagavad Gitā and the Brahmasutras. The different schools of thought by *āchāryas* like Shankarāchārya,

Rāmānujāchārya, etc. were established and recognized by their commentaries on the Prasthānatraya.

17. What is the Vachanāmrut?

Vachanāmrut is the sacred religious text of the Swaminarayan Sampradāya, which is a compilation of the discourses of Bhagwan Swaminarayan. The content of the Vachanāmrut is theological, philosophical and spiritual. It deals with the nature of *jiva, ishwara, māyā,* Brahman and Parabrahman. It also includes the principles of *moksha*, the indispensability of guru, happiness, misery, non-violence, prayer, bhakti, morals, good company, service, positive attitude, introspection, dhyan and many other practical aspects of daily life and spiritual sadhana.

Bhagwan Swaminarayan often quoted and gave references of the Vedas, Upanishads, Rāmāyana, Mahābhārata, Bhagavad Gitā, Shrimad Bhāgavata and other shastras during his discourses. The Vachanāmrut is a distillation of the Hindu sacred texts in its simplest and palatable form.

GLOSSARY

A

āchāra	code of conduct
āchāryas	establisher of a religious doctrine or a school of philosophy. The later āchāryas, starting with Shankarāchārya, established a school of philosophy, having written commentaries on the Brahmasutras, the Upanishads and the Bhagavad Gitā
adharma	unrighteousness
adhvaryu	special priest of Yajur Veda
ādikāvya	first poem, namely the Rāmāyana
agni	fire
Anubhāshya	Vallabhāchārya's commentary on the Brahmasutras
apaurusheya	not man-made (normally referring to Vedas)
Archajyotisha	a 36-verse book on astrology available from the early sections of the Rig Veda
arghya	offering of water in a ritual
artha	one of the four human endeavours allowing for the fulfilment of desires for material objects, in particular wealth

Arthashāstra	writings dealing with economics and politics. One such work is Kautilya's *Arthashāstra*
Ashtādhyāyi	Sanskrit grammar text by Pānini
āstika	1. 'Believer'. Person who believes in the existence of God, or more generally, one who is religiously inclined. 2. Person or shastra that accept the authority and authenticity of the Vedas
astra	a missile. It is presided over by a particular deva and when invoked it empowers the missile with destructive capability
Atharvajyotisha	book on astrology from the Vedic period
ātmā	pure soul
avidyā	synonymous with *māyā*. False understanding of the nature of reality. Ignorance

B

bhaktisutras	aphorisms on bhakti by Nārada and Shāndilya
bhāshya	commentary or intepretation of the Hindu shastras
bhuta-runa	debt to all living beings including birds, animals, etc.
bhuta-yajna	caring for and nourishing all life forms

brahmacharya	practice of eight-fold celibacy and being immersed in Brahman (Paramātmā)
brahmanishtha	God-realized
brahmavidyā	spiritual knowledge
brahma-yajna	repaying one's debt to the rishi or guru by meditating on God, listening to spiritual discourses, having darshan of God, reading the shastras, partaking of food that has been offered to God, and by contemplating on and praying to God.

C

chandas	prosody
chopāi	verses in a shastra that are mostly sung, like in Rāmāyana

D

daivata kānda	book that explains names of deities
dāna	donation in cash or kind
darbār	a person of Kshatriya class. A Kshatriya's house
dehabhāva	attachment to the physical body. Misidentification of one's self with the body
deva-runa	debt to devas (gods)
devatā	deva
deva-yajna	fire sacrifice to appease the devas
dikshā	initiation

divya	divine. Deciding upon a matter in dispute through an ordeal like giving *visha* (poison), *koshāpana, phāla,* etc.
divya dampati	divine couple

E

ekāntika dharma	dharma or religion that comprises four aspects, namely, dharma, *jnāna, vairagya* and bhakti

G

gandharvas	class of celestial deities whose occupation is music and singing; musicians of heaven
gruhasthāshrama	the householder stage, one of four stages of life
guru-shishya	master-disciple

H

Halāyudhakosha	Sanskrit dictionary
hotā	priest of the Rig Veda who recites mantras during fire sacrifice or *yajna* to invoke the devas for receiving the oblations

I

ishtāpurta	cumulative result of performance of sacrificial rites and good works for others

itihāsa	epics like the Rāmāyana and Mahābhārata

J

jagat	world
jiva	self or soul
jivātmā	see *jiva*
jnāna	knowledge
jnāna-kānda	knowledge section
jnāni	a wise person

K

kāma	one of the four human endeavours allowing for the regulated fulfilment of one's personal and social desires
kānda	section
kapha	phlegm
kriyā	movement or activity
kundalini shakti	basic power in a human being which is likened to a coiled serpent lying dormant at the *mulādhāra* until it is roused by appropriate yogic exercises

M

madya	wine
maithuna	sexual intercourse
manavantara	time ruled by one Manu, which is 308 million human years

mandala	book or group
matsya	fish
moha	excessive attraction or attachment to people, relatives and objects
moksha	liberation from *māyā* and cycle of birth and deaths, leading to experience of divine bliss
mudrā	posture
murti	sacred image of God or deity
murti-pujā	worship of a *murti*

N

naraka	hell
Nāsadiyasukta	hymn of cosmic creation in the Rig Veda
Nighantu	dictionary of difficult Vedic words
nirukta	oldest Indian treatise on etymology, philology and semantics. One of the six Vedāngas
nishedha	prohibitions or don'ts
nishkāma	celibacy. Desirelessness
nitya mukta	eternally liberated soul
nru-runa	debt to human beings
nru-yajna	service to humanity

P

pāda	chapter
pancha-mahāyajnas	five *yajnas*: *deva-yajna, rishi-yajna, pitru-*

yajna, nru-yajna and *bhuta-yajna*

pancha-makāra   Vāmāchāra or left-hand path promotes the ritual use of "five Ms", namely, wine *(madya)*, fish *(matsya)*, meat *(māmsa)*, posture *(mudrā)* and extramarital sexual union *(maithuna)*

paramhansas   'supreme swan'. A male sadhu of the highest order, characterized by his ability to discriminate between *sat* and *asat* – just as swans were traditionally considered to be able to separate milk from water

pariprashna   questioning the guru and asking for clarification of spiritual principles

parva   chapter in shastra. Celebration

pashu   soul

pinda   rice ball

pingala   shastra that deals with versification or the rules for the metres in which Vedic mantras and poems were composed

pitru runa   debt to ancestors

pitru   forefather

pitru-yajna   yajna performed to please one's ancestors

pitta   bile

prajnā   wisdom

pranipāta   surrendering to guru

pratisarga   dissolution and re-creation *(pratisarga)*

of the universe

prāyashchitta	atonement for moral lapses
purushārtha	pursuits. Collective term for the four goals legitimately pursued by all Hindus, namely: dharma (duties), *artha* (material wealth), *kāma* (desires), and ultimately, *moksha* (liberation)
Purushasukta	hymn of the Ultimate Reality in the Rig Veda

R

rāga	tune, mode of music
rājya	kingdom
rishi-yajna	indebtedness to the rishis or sages, who gave us the legacy of spirituality, culture and education. This debt can be repaid by studying the sacred texts, teaching them to the next generation, practising their principles, and performing the samskaras and austerities prescribed by the sages. Also known as *brahma-yajna*
ruchās or ruks	hymns or sacred verses
runa	obligation
runa-traya	three-fold debts or obligations, namely, *deva-runa* (debt to gods), *rishi-runa* (debt to sages) and *pitru runa* (debt to ancestors)
ruta	cosmic order

S

sādhaka	a person endeavouring on the spiritual path. An aspirant or a novice on the spiritual path
saguna upāsanā	worship of the Supreme Reality having a form and qualities
sāman	tune in which Vedic hymns are sung
sampradāya	a tradition handed down from a founder through successive spiritual gurus
Sānkhyasutras	text which contain the aphorisms of Sānkhya philosophy. The one available today is believed to have been written later in the name of Sage Kapila
sannyastāshrama	complete renunciation of worldly activities and responsibilities to fully engage oneself in meditation and other spiritual sadhanas; the fourth stage of life
sapta svara	seven notes in Indian music
satya	truth
sevā	service
shabda	word. Testimony
shastravidyā	science of weaponry
shloka	Sanskrit verse
shrāddha	rites to propitiate one's ancestors
Shribhāshya	Rāmānujāchārya's commentary on the Brahmasutras
shrotriya	one who knows and has realized the true meaning of the shastras

Shruti	'that which is heard' or revealed. Refers to Veda
Smrutis	'that which is remembered'. Refers to Smruti Shastras, namely, Dharma Shastras, Purānas and Itihāsa, etc.
sthapati	architect
suktas	hymn
sutras	aphorism
swādhyāya	self-study
swarga	abode of the devas

U

udgātā	special priest of Sāma Veda
upādāna	material cause (of world)

V

vairagya	detachment from material objects and pursuits
Vaisheshikasutras	book of aphorisms on Vaisheshika philosophy by Sage Kanāda
vānaprasthāshrama	third of the four stages of life, when one withdraws to some extent from social duties and serves merely as an elderly advisor. Literally implying 'taking to the forests'
vāta	air in body
vidhi	ritual act. The 'do's' codes of conduct
vidyā	knowledge

vishāda	sadness
vyavahāra	social and financial dealings

Y

yajna	fire ritual
yajna kunda	pit to perform *yagna*
yajna vedi	altar for performing *yagna*
yajus	Yajur Veda